# PSYCHOLOGY
### *of* ADOLESCENCE
### *for* TEACHERS

# Psychology of Adolescence for Teachers

GLENN MYERS BLAIR AND R. STEWART JONES

# PSYCHOLOGY
## *of* ADOLESCENCE
## *for* TEACHERS

1344

### *by* *Glenn Myers Blair*

PROFESSOR OF EDUCATIONAL PSYCHOLOGY
UNIVERSITY OF ILLINOIS

### *and* *R. Stewart Jones*

CHAIRMAN, DEPARTMENT OF EDUCATIONAL PSYCHOLOGY
UNIVERSITY OF ILLINOIS

THE MACMILLAN COMPANY, NEW YORK
COLLIER-MACMILLAN LIMITED, LONDON

THE MACMILLAN COMPANY, NEW YORK
COLLIER-MACMILLAN CANADA, LTD., TORONTO, ONTARIO

Printed in the United States of America

# Preface

A very substantial proportion of the members of every society are in that phase of development which we call adolescence. The exact proportion, of course, varies considerably from culture to culture and, in the same culture, with different periods of time. Those societies, such as ours, which prolong the transition period between childhood and adulthood have exceptionally high percentages of adolescents. Certain primitive societies which quickly mature their children into adults have at any given time a much smaller percentage. In our own culture in pioneer days, the proportion of individuals who would have been labeled adolescent would be much smaller than at the present time. In this earlier period of our history, individuals married while relatively young and took on adult responsibilities which are today reserved for much older people.

The period of adolescence has been widely studied since the time of G. Stanley Hall. The tendency today is to attribute much more of the adolescent's behavior to social factors than formerly. The findings of cultural anthropologists, who have studied adolescents in primitive societies and at different social levels in our own society, have been particularly effective in contributing to the present point of view. The biological basis of adolescent behavior is still deemed to be of importance, but increased emphasis is now being placed upon the social-cultural determiners of behavior.

The adolescent has special problems that he did not have as a child and that are somewhat different from those he will encounter as an adult. He has certain pressing needs which must be met, and a series of developmental tasks and problems which he must master if he is to become a self-sufficient member of society.

This book is designed for teachers and prospective teachers as well as for others who are concerned with the education of adolescents. Our junior and senior high schools are crowded with youngsters who need the specialized help which only enlightened educators can give. Probably at no time in our history is there greater need for efficiency in teaching. It is hoped that this book will provide teachers with many of the insights needed for carrying out their work.

The authors are indebted to the thousands of teachers in their classes at the University of Illinois who have provided ideas and helpful suggestions for this book. Credit should also go to the many research workers and colleagues in psychology and related fields who have contributed the experimental evidence upon which the book is based.

GLENN M. BLAIR
R. STEWART JONES

URBANA, ILLINOIS

# Contents

# 1

# The Adolescent Period

ADOLESCENCE IS that period in every person's life which lies between the end of childhood and the beginning of adulthood. It may be a long period or a short one. It varies in length from family to family, from one socio-economic level to another, and from culture to culture. Its length may even fluctuate in the same society from time to time, depending upon economic or other conditions.

Some primitive societies mature their children into adults almost overnight and thus practically eliminate the adolescent period. In present-day America, however, adolescence usually covers a long, drawn-out span of years.

A girl or boy in a middle-class American family may spend as long as ten years making the transition from childhood to adulthood. An example of this would be a girl who menstruates at twelve, thus ending her childhood, and then continues to be a dependent member of her family until she marries at twenty-two. During this ten-year span she may attend junior high school, senior high school, and college. All this time she is in the process of getting weaned from the family and becoming an independent adult. The same general pattern holds for the boy who may exhibit his first pubic hair at thirteen and then not leave the family nest until twenty-three. Girls usually begin the adolescent period a year or two earlier than boys, and similarly may finish it a year or two earlier.

In lower-class American families young people are typically "put on their own" much sooner than in middle-class families.

1

These adolescents may thus have only four or five years to spend in the so-called "difficult period" known as adolescence. Many lower-class youths drop out of high school before graduation and leave home, and some even set up families of their own by the time they are seventeen or eighteen.

Every teacher should be aware of the fact that children in the same family or society may vary greatly with respect to the age at which they begin adolescence. Fourth- and fifth-grade teachers often report that they have girls in their classes who have reached puberty and who physically resemble young women while the rest of the class members are immature children. (The special adjustment problems of early- and later-maturing children will be treated in a later section of this book.)

## Adolescence—Biological or Social

Adolescence is both biological and social in nature. The beginning of adolescence is marked by biological changes in girls and boys. As a matter of fact, just before puberty there occurs what is known as a pre-adolescent growth spurt. It takes place in girls mostly during the ages of nine to twelve, and in boys between eleven and fourteen. Prior to this time, the rate of growth in height and weight has been slowing down. Now, for a two- or three-year period the rate is greatly accelerated. During this period, and following shortly thereafter, the secondary sexual characteristics emerge. In girls there is typically first the rounding out of the hips, then breast development, the appearance of pubic hair, and menstruation. Typically, the American girl first menstruates when she is about thirteen. Most American girls menstruate initially between the ages of eleven and fifteen. Only 3 per cent menstruate earlier than this, and 3 per cent later. The effect of environmental factors on menstruation, however, has been noted. Data show that girls in the United States menstruate earlier than those in other parts of the world. Also, girls today in America are reaching the menarche a few months earlier than did their mothers. Furthermore, girls from the middle classes menstruate earlier than do girls from the lower socio-economic classes in America. The environmental factors responsible for these differences are not definitely known at this time, but it is believed that better diet and health, and changed habits of activity may have something to do with them.

In boys, some of the secondary sexual characteristics that mark the beginning of adolescence are appearance of pubic hair, facial hair, and change of voice. These are all biologically induced.

The end of adolescence for both girls and boys is marked largely by social changes and criteria. Such factors as when an adolescent leaves home, gets a job, and can vote determine when his transition from childhood to adulthood is accomplished. The length of the period is thus primarily a social phenomenon.

The problems adolescents face during the long period of growing up have both biological and social roots. Physical changes and deviations can create problems. Society also creates problems for adolescents. Adolescents in America behave very differently than do adolescents in Samoa or New Guinea. Adolescents in the American middle class show markedly different personality characteristics than do those in the lower classes.

The teacher who would help adolescents make good adjustments to school and to life should understand the nature and effects of both biological and social factors in adolescent development.

## Why Adolescence Requires Special Study

The general principles of psychology, as they relate to growth, learning, and adjustment, apply to individuals at the adolescent stage as well as to those in any other phase of development. For example, a good course in social psychology, mental hygiene, or learning should help the secondary school teacher deal with adolescents. Yet each stage of life has special and unique problems which must be understood if applications of psychological principles are to be appropriate. The teacher who works with adolescents needs to understand, among other things, the nature of the transition period through which adolescents pass, the special needs and developmental tasks of adolescents, the role of the peer group in influencing adolescent behavior, the effects of somatic variations on adolescent behavior, the special problems arising out of family life, causes of adolescent delinquency, and special problems arising out of sexual maturation. Many of the problems an adolescent faces are new to him and are ones which he may not encounter again if he makes a successful adjustment to them.

## The Adolescent Transition Period

There are a number of transition or crisis periods in the life span of every individual. For example, the child who goes to school and leaves the security of his home behind for the first time is facing a special crisis period and must make suitable adjustments. At the other end of life, the man who retires from his job faces a crucial period for which radical adjustments must be made. Adolescence represents one of the greatest of these periods of crisis. In making the jump from childhood to adulthood, great strain and confusion sometimes results.

The psychologist, Kurt Lewin, has held that the adolescent is really in a "no-man's land." He is neither a child nor an adult, but is caught in a field of overlapping forces and expectations (see Figure 1). The child's role is clearly structured. He knows what he can and cannot do. The adult likewise understands pretty well what his role is. The adolescent, however, is in an ambigu-

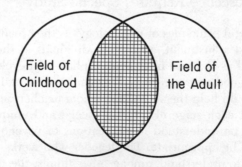

Figure 1.   The psychological field of the adolescent is the dark space where the two circles overlap.

ous position. He never really knows how he stands. One moment he is told by his parents that he is too young to take the family car out of town. The next moment he is chided for not acting like a man and is told that he is as big as his father. It is believed that this uncertainty as to his role causes many an adolescent to be in conflict—to vacillate, to be sensitive and sometimes unstable and unpredictable.

It is a well-known fact that delinquency rates soar during the period of adolescence, that suicides become increasingly prevalent, that drug and alcohol addiction may have their beginning, and that much general unhappiness exists. Adolescence is also a period when satisfactory heterosexual adjustments are facilitated or hindered, when careers are planned, and when philosophies of life become molded. Teachers who understand adolescents and the problems they encounter can do much to help them make a successful transition to adult status. Too often, however, it seems that schools and teachers, because of lack of understanding, actually frustrate adolescents and contribute to their general maladjustment.

## Developmental Tasks of Adolescence

The term "developmental tasks," used earlier in this chapter, refers to those problems that individuals typically face at different periods of their life development. The infant or small child must master the complexities of learning to walk, learning to talk, and controlling the elimination of waste products of the body. In middle childhood such skills as learning to play games and learning to read become of major importance. So far as adolescents are concerned, the developmental tasks represent the vital problems which must be met and solved during the transition from childhood to adulthood. These problems are not entirely unique to the adolescent period, but they are ones upon which the adolescent must work if he eventually expects to achieve a successful adult role. Robert Havighurst, in his book *Human Development and Education,* has listed ten tasks that are particularly significant for the adolescent and that need much attention during this period: (1) achieving new and more mature relations with age mates of both sexes, (2) achieving a masculine or feminine social role,

(3) accepting one's physique and using the body effectively, (4) achieving emotional independence of parents and other adults, (5) achieving assurance of economic independence, (6) selecting and preparing for an occupation, (7) preparing for marriage and family life, (8) developing intellectual skills and concepts necessary for civic competence, (9) desiring and achieving socially responsible behavior, and (10) acquiring a set of values and an ethical system as a guide to behavior.

If these are, indeed, the important problems of adolescence, schools should gear their curricula to take them into account. The school has traditionally devoted most of its energy to helping the adolescent develop his intellectual skills. This is perhaps as it should be. However, such tasks as achieving socially responsible behavior and preparing for marriage and family life, as well as other tasks on this list, should not be neglected.

## Readings for Further Study

Blair, Glenn M., "What Teachers Should Know About the Psychology of Adolescence," *Journal of Educational Psychology*, Vol. 41, pp. 356–361.

Coleman, James S., *The Adolescent Society*. New York: Glencoe Free Press, 1961.

Davis, Kingsley, "Adolescence and the Social Structure," Chapter 4 in J. M. Seidman, ed., *The Adolescent—A Book of Readings*, rev. ed. New York: Holt, Rinehart & Winston, 1960.

Havighurst, Robert J., *Human Development and Education*. New York: Longmans, Green and Co., 1953, Chapters 9–15.

Horrocks, John E., *The Psychology of Adolescence*, 2nd ed. Boston: Houghton Mifflin Co., 1962, Chapter 1.

Lewin, Kurt, "The Field Theory Approach to Adolescence," Chapter 3 in J. M. Seidman, ed., *The Adolescent—A Book of Readings*, rev. ed. New York: Holt, Rinehart & Winston, 1960.

Luchins, Abraham S., "On the Theories and Problems of Adolescence," in Noll and Noll, eds., *Readings in Educational Psychology*. New York: The Macmillan Co., 1962, pp. 102–120.

Mead, Margaret, *From the South Seas*. New York: William Morrow & Co., 1939.

Muuss, Rolf E., *Theories of Adolescence*. New York: Random House, 1962.

# 2

# Adolescent Needs and Processes of Adjustment

THE ADOLESCENT, like everyone else, spends twenty-four hours a day satisfying or attempting to satisfy his physical, social, and personality needs. Whether he is shy, aggressive, negativistic, reckless, idealistic, helpful, conforming, or impudent depends upon which needs are active and how he goes about satisfying them. All behavior can be said to be motivated. The thoughtful teacher should continually ask the question, "What need of this adolescent is being met by this particular mode of behavior?" Needs may be satisfied in numerous ways. Some may be socially acceptable; others may lead to social difficulties for the adolescent. One of the chief responsibilities of teachers and schools should be to help young people satisfy their biological and acquired needs in ways which will be socially and personally rewarding.

## Physical Needs of Adolescents

Adolescents the world over possess much the same biological and tissue needs. These are sometimes referred to as biogenic needs. They include hunger, thirst, activity, rest, sex, temperature regulation, evacuation (urination and defecation), and avoidance of physical injury. The way these needs are met, however, vary greatly in different parts of the world. For exam-

7

ple, the thirsty adolescent in Italy would probably drink wine, whereas an American youth might prefer a "coke." To satisfy the need for activity, a Cuban youth might engage in the game of *jai alai,* but his American counterpart would probably be much more interested in basketball.

Sex needs of youth are also handled quite differently in various countries of the world and in different subcultures in our own society. In Thailand, for example, young people of high school age would never be allowed to engage in mixed social dancing, but in America our schools feel that school dances provide a very valuable outlet for both boys and girls. In American middle-class society, premarital sexual intercourse is strongly frowned upon; in American lower-class society, attitudes toward such behavior are more permissive, and the behavior may even be condoned. (Sex problems of American adolescents and programs for sex education in our secondary schools will be dealt with later in this book.)

Although teachers should understand the nature of the physical needs of young people, it is perhaps even more important that they thoroughly understand and take into account the social and personality needs of youth.

## Personality Needs of Adolescents

Among the human personality needs that are particularly urgent during adolescence are the needs for status, independence, achievement, and a satisfying philosophy of life.

Perhaps no need is more important for the adolescent than the *need for status.* He wants to be important, to have standing in his group, to be recognized as a person of worth. He craves to achieve adult status and leave behind the insignia of childhood. Thus, it is not at all uncommon to see adolescent boys smoking cigarettes and acting in other ways which seem to them to be grown up and sophisticated. The adolescent girl wants to wear high-heeled shoes, use lipstick, and take on the ways of adult women. Status in the peer group is probably more important to many adolescents than status in the eyes of their parents or teachers, yet recognition from both of these sources is cherished by adolescents. The teacher who directs the activities of the adolescent should always ask himself whether or not the experiences of the classroom are status-producing ones for each individual. The adolescent who is achieving his goals in school and is accorded appropriate recognition is seldom, if ever, a disciplinary problem. Furthermore, he is in the best possible emotional state to continue to profit from the learning experiences of the school.

One of the authors observed the classroom of a teacher who delighted in forcing her pupils, especially boys, to read poetry aloud. Most of the boys were fourteen or fifteen years of age— just at the time when they were trying to throw off the label of "children" and to avoid "sissy" activities. The teacher asked them to read aloud Poe's "The Bells." One section of the poem read, "to the tintinnabulation that so musically wells from the bells, bells, bells, bells, bells, bells, bells." The teacher insisted that each boy rise and read this phrase with different volume and inflection on each "bells." Finally, one of the larger boys could stand it no longer. He slammed his book on the floor in disgust and stamped out of the classroom.

This teacher did not realize how sensitive adolescents are about being treated like youngsters or having to engage in activities they feel to be below their dignity. There is probably no surer way for any teacher to become unpopular with a group of teenagers than for her to call them children or to imply in any other way that they are anything but young men and women.

A second personality need which takes on increasing significance and importance during adolescence is the *need for independence*. The adolescent craves to be weaned from parental restrictions and to become a self-directing person. He wants his own room in the home, where he can be free from younger members of the family and can do his own thinking and plan his own activities. He would like a lock on the door and a private telephone if possible. He desires to run his own life. Young children have no objection to their parents' visiting school and inquiring about their progress, but many adolescents object to this practice, because it implies that they cannot handle their own affairs. The adolescent boy who is a member of the tennis or basketball team in high school usually prefers that his parents, if they attend the matches or games, be not too conspicuous. The normal adolescent does not want anyone to sense or faintly suspect that he is in any way tied to his mother's apron strings.

One of the authors knows of a high school girl whose mother brings her to school every day and insists on helping her carry her books to her locker. On a day that grades were given out, the mother stayed the whole day and visited each class with her daughter. According to the school counselor, this girl is on the verge of a nervous breakdown because of the overprotectiveness of the mother.

Teachers can also be too overprotective of their adolescent students. There is no reason why young people in their teens cannot help plan their programs of instruction, help set up rules for classroom conduct, and take on other responsibilities in line with their increased abilities and maturity levels. Yet, too often, high school teachers "spoon-feed" their students, scold them for little misbehaviors, plan their work for them, and expect little in the way of responsible behavior. If that is what teachers expect that is what they usually get. Adolescents who are treated in a more adult manner will show a more adult behavior, and can be depended upon to take on and carry out highly independent and responsible assignments.

Closely related to these two personality needs is the *need for achievement*. So far as learning is concerned, this need is of paramount importance. Thorndike, Hull, and Skinner, all leading learning theorists of our time, hold that learning is most effectively accomplished when a student's efforts are followed by a sense of achievement (reinforcement). The way to get pupils to learn rapidly and to like their schoolwork is to take notice of good work that they do. Every pupil at times does something that is worthy of commendation. This should be called to the attention of the student, and perhaps to other members of the class. Slow learners particularly, or adolescents who are not interested in school, need successful experiences if they are to make any worthwhile progress.

Threats and punishments have sometimes been used in efforts to get pupils to study, but this approach may have many bad side effects. The student may learn a little geometry, but at the same time he may learn to hate the teacher and the subject. Numerous experimental studies have shown the superiority of praise over censure as a motivating device in producing learning.

In utilizing this need for achievement, which is present in all pupils, the teacher should carefully gear the classroom activities to the current achievement levels of each individual student. Only in this way can the classroom atmosphere be truly conducive to learning. First-grade teachers and some elementary teachers make an effort to apply this famous principle of readiness, but secondary school teachers quite generally neglect to so differentiate the work in their classes that each student can be a successful achiever.

The final personality need of adolescents (to be mentioned at this point) is the *need for a satisfying philosophy of life*. The young child asks many questions and does some immature speculating about the nature of the universe, but it is not until adolescence that he exhibits a persistent and driving concern about the meaning of life. The adolescent is concerned with questions about truth, religion, and ideals. He has a desire for *closure*. He wants the gaps in his knowledge about the purposes of life to be filled. A satisfying philosophy or set of beliefs tends to provide him psychological security. Data show that in adolescence religious conversion and initial radical political activity reach a peak. Dictators who establish youth movements and religious organizations which sponsor young peoples' societies recognize the importance of this period for attitude formation. The school has a great responsibility to help the adolescent find himself and develop the outlooks on life that are consistent with our democratic philosophy and that will give him stability of character and a sense of security.

## How Needs Operate

When a need exists and is unsatisfied, the adolescent becomes restless and tense. He seeks some goal which will reduce the state of imbalance that exists within him. If he is hungry, he seeks food; if he is tired, he craves rest; if he is unnoticed, he strives for attention and status. If the adolescent is overprotected, he will make an attempt to secure independence. When a need is completely satisfied, a temporary state of equilibrium is established, and activity toward the appropriate goal ceases. A student who has been complimented by his teacher or peers for some worthy performance may not need further vocal approval for several hours or even days. He does, however, need to feel constantly that he belongs, has status, and is a worthwhile person. Most of the personality needs remain in a somewhat unsatisfied state. Seldom does an adolescent—or anyone else, for that matter—achieve too much status, achievement, or psychological security.

## Conditions Creating Frustration

There are two types of situations that create frustration. The first arises from blocked goals; the second comes from incompatible goals held by the individual.

The adolescent who seeks the satisfaction of his basic needs frequently finds himself blocked in reaching them. Laws that discriminate between races, requirements of admission to certain courses or schools, and strictly imposed standards of appropriate dress are all examples of situations that may cause frustration for some adolescents. School regulations which insist that all pupils meet certain prescribed levels of achievement may be very thwarting to pupils of limited background or ability. Poverty may seriously limit what an adolescent may do. The student with a personal defect or physical ailment may not be able to engage in activities open to others.

As has been suggested, conflict and frustration also inevitably ensue when the individual strives to attain two incompatible goals. The student who tries to be a playboy and an honor student at the same time may run into difficulties, as will also the student who attempts to please two groups that have widely differing ideals. Frequently an adolescent's moral standards, which have been developed as a child, come in conflict with the patterns of behavior of his school friends. He may have been taught that it is wrong to smoke, dance, play cards, or attend movies. When he secretly engages in such activities, he may have severe guilt feelings.

The adolescent whose needs are thwarted or who is in conflict is tense and uncomfortable. He is in a state of imbalance. He must make some adjustment in order to reduce this state of hypertension and make the situation tolerable for himself. Teachers should understand the types of adjustment mechanisms employed by adolescents whose needs go unmet. These include aggression (direct and indirect), compensation, identification, rationalization, projection, reaction formation, egocentrism, negativism, withdrawal, and development of physical ailments.

## Typical Adjustment Mechanisms

### AGGRESSION

This may be either direct or indirect. High school pupils have physically attacked school teachers who have humiliated them or thwarted them in the attainment of their goals. Sometimes, however, the maladjusted pupil will instead release his hostile feelings toward a teacher by fighting a fellow student or by breaking street lights. Some of the socially acceptable channels that can be used by the school for relieving aggressive feelings include athletic contests and dramatic plays.

### COMPENSATION

Every adolescent must feel important. If he cannot attain distinction one way, he will try to attain it another. The boy who is a failure in algebra may save his ego or self-esteem by excelling in athletics. The boy who cannot dance may brag of his prowess with girls, and the pupil who is never given any scholastic recognition may attain distinction as the school's biggest rowdy. Attainable goals are substituted for nonattainable goals, or goals difficult to attain. Teachers should help pupils find activities in which they can excel and thus compensate for whatever weaknesses they may possess.

## IDENTIFICATION

The unsuccessful adolescent can gain some measure of reflected glory by associating with successful students. A common sight around a high school is a nonathletic youth walking side by side with a successful athlete, or at least trailing close behind. Identification can become a powerful dynamism in the formation of personality and character. The school by providing worthwhile models in the form of teachers, personages in literature and science, and appropriate school traditions, can do much to assist pupils in making proper identifications.

## RATIONALIZATION

It is difficult for a student to admit that he has failed to reach his goals. He may excuse his shortcomings by maintaining that the goal was not important anyway, or that his teachers were unfair. This is known as the sour-grapes mechanism. Another form of rationalization is known as the sweet-lemon, or Pollyanna, mechanism. The pupil may be unsatisfied with his level of achievement but maintain that everything is lovely. For example, if he is given a minor part in a school play, he may be secretly disappointed but loudly proclaim that it is just the role he wanted. Rationalization, though used by everyone to maintain mental health, should not be overused. Teachers should help pupils face up to their problems and not always rationalize them away.

## PROJECTION

Another method used by students to excuse their shortcomings and relieve guilt feelings is known as projection. This is a mechanism by which an individual ascribes to others his own weaknesses, faults, and impulses. An adolescent who himself cheats may conclude that everyone does. He judges others by himself. Although projection is extremely common and undoubtedly reduces tension in a frustrated individual, constant reliance on it is by no means to be commended. Teachers should aid adolescents to make adjustments that will protect and enhance their egos in ways other than those which involve projection.

## REACTION FORMATION

An adolescent conflict may sometimes be resolved by strengthening one of the conflicting motives. The motive which induces anxiety is repressed, and the opposite one is given full reign. The student who is extremely prudish, inordinately polite, or outstandingly sanctimonious may actually be covering up for powerful feelings in the other direction. A high school boy, for example, may declare that it is disgraceful for boys and girls to have dates or walk around arm in arm. Actually, this is exactly what he would like to do if his conscience would permit it, or if he could get a girl friend.

## EGOCENTRISM

The adolescent who feels insecure will often strive to establish himself as the center of attention. He may show off, ask numerous questions, talk loudly, and try to be witty. One of the authors knows of a ninth-grade youngster who released a snake in the back of the room while his English class was in session. Needless to say, he received attention not only from his classmates but also from his teacher, who soon arrived on the scene. This particular boy had been very unsuccessful in English, largely because of low scholastic ability and poor home background. Since no provision was made in this class for individual differences in ability and achievement, there were few ways, if any, that he could attract attention through normal channels. Engaging in this type of prank was, however, well within his abilities, and it gave him a feeling of importance.

## NEGATIVISM

Another ego-enhancing and attention-getting device is known as negativism. The adolescent may be opposed to almost everything. In school, when a group decides upon a course of action, the negativistic adolescent may stubbornly refuse to go along with the decision. He will often sulk, rebel against authority, and refuse to be bound by rules. The wise teacher will quickly diagnose such behavior as being symptomatic of a frustrated pupil whose needs are being thwarted.

## WITHDRAWAL

In the face of thwarting and distressing situations, some pupils find that the easiest way out is to withdraw. The boy who has failed in school may indulge in excessive daydreaming. He may imagine that he is a successful boat captain or aviator. The girl who has failed to get any dates for school dances may sit for hours dreaming of her success as a dancer or opera singer. The pupil who habitually achieves his satisfactions in the world of fantasy is in for trouble.

## ESCAPE THROUGH PHYSICAL AILMENTS

The adolescent who is in conflict or who faces a difficult school situation may sometimes make a graceful withdrawal by developing what are sometimes referred to as *hysteroid reactions*. On the day of an examination he may become so ill that he has to return home; the next day he is perfectly well. Teachers should be sympathetic to pupils who develop headaches, eye trouble, sinus trouble, colds, sore throats, and fainting spells in their attempts to avoid unpleasant and painful school experiences. In a school where every pupil can achieve success, such problems rarely arise.

## Readings for Further Study

Baller, Warren R., *Readings in the Psychology of Human Growth and Development*. New York: Holt, Rinehart & Winston, 1962, Chapter 6.

Blair, Glenn M., Jones, R. Stewart, and Simpson, Ray H., *Educational Psychology*, 2nd ed. New York: The Macmillan Co., 1962, Chapter 13.

Coleman, James C., *Personality Dynamics and Effective Behavior*. Chicago: Scott, Foresman and Co., 1960, Chapters 5, 6.
Hountras, Peter T., ed. *Mental Hygiene—A Text of Readings*. Columbus, Ohio: Charles E. Merrill Co., 1961, Chapters 25–28.
Shaffer, Laurance F., and Shoben, Edward J., *The Psychology of Adjustment*, 2nd ed. Boston: Houghton Mifflin Co., 1956, Chapters 6–10.
Thorpe, Louis P., *The Psychology of Mental Health*, 2nd ed. New York: Ronald Press Co., 1960, Chapters 2, 3.

# 3

# The Adolescent and Social Class

IN AMERICA, as in other parts of the world, people are grouped into social classes. Anthropologists have shown that there is no tribe, race, or civilization anywhere that is classless—where everyone is on an equal footing with everyone else. In Europe for centuries young people of different social classes have gone to different schools. In America the same practice prevails in many sections of the country. On the eastern seaboard, for example, pupils from extremely wealthy homes (upper class) go to certain exclusive private schools. Some parents with less wealth and social position, but who are in the upper-middle class, also send their children to private schools. The public school system in many eastern industrial centers caters primarily to pupils in the lower-middle class and lower classes.

In the Midwest and far West, however, private schools are much fewer in number, and a tradition seems to exist that it is all right for pupils of widely different social classes to attend the same public junior or senior high schools. Of course, in certain exclusive neighborhoods near large cities, most of the pupils in the local public school come from the upper or upper-middle classes. Upon high school graduation many of them will receive new cars as graduation gifts. In slum neighborhoods the pupils will be almost entirely from the lower classes. Many will not even finish high school, and there will be no large gifts for those who do.

In the smaller cities and rural areas of America, however, particularly west of the Alleghenies, public secondary school teachers frequently have in their classes, sitting side by side, pupils from upper, middle, and lower classes.

Until relatively recently, it was not generally realized that American society had a somewhat rigid social structure. But such studies as W. Lloyd Warner's *Yankee City*, August B. Hollingshead's *Elmtown's Youth*, and Barker and Wright's *Midwest and Its Children* have shown that this is the case. These and other studies have also shown that great differences exist between the attitudes, behavior, and value systems of adolescents in the different social classes. Teachers should know about these differences in order to deal effectively with the pupils they instruct. Since most of the young people of America belong to the middle or lower classes (only about 2 per cent in the upper classes), the discussion which follows will be devoted primarily to summarizing some of the characteristics of middle- and lower-class adolescents. The differences in behavior between middle-class and lower-class adolescents are, of course, learned. They are ways of acting and thinking that are derived from the families and other social groups of which the young people are members.

## Differences Between Middle-Class and Lower-Class Adolescents

### ATTITUDES TOWARD SCHOOL

No social group in America is more impressed with the importance of an education than is the middle class. This group feels that education is power. The young people who come from the middle class are urged by their parents to finish high school, go on to college, and in a great many instances pursue graduate study. The long-term goals of many middle-class youngsters include entering such professions as teaching, the ministry, medicine, and executive positions in business. As a matter of fact, often greater pressure is exerted on adolescents in the middle class to get an excellent education than on upper-class adolescents.

Middle-class parents, as a rule, are constantly concerned about the scholastic records of their children, attend PTA meetings regularly, visit the schools, save money for their children's college education, and in general leave no stone unturned in attempting to assure success for their children in the educational venture.

Lower-class society, on the other hand, puts little premium on education. Parents will, at times, encourage truancy, belittle education, and show slight or no interest in PTA work or their child's scholastic progress. As a result, many adolescents from the lower class desire to leave school as soon as possible. They want to get a job, get married (or at least find a common-law partner), make some money immediately, and get on with living. They do not see the relevance of the academically oriented school program to their plans.

Teachers are thus faced with a very severe motivation problem so far as many lower-class adolescents are concerned. Courses in shop work, carpentry, beauty culture, and the like may appeal to some, but the college preparatory subjects may leave them unimpressed.

There is, of course, mobility in our social structure. One does not have to remain indefinitely in the social class of his parents; he can move upward. The American school is perhaps the greatest single agency for promoting a desire on the part of pupils to move from the lower to the middle class. Many pupils from the lower class identify with their middle-class teachers and eventually develop the attitudes and goals of the middle class. Perhaps one of the purposes of education and teaching should be to facilitate this process. In any event, teachers who work with adolescents from the lower class must recognize that a real problem of motivation may exist and that success as a teacher may depend upon how well this problem is met.

## ATTITUDES TOWARD AGGRESSION

Middle-class youth are typically taught by parents that fistfighting is nonproductive—that a clever person can avoid violence in solving personal disputes. Lower-class youngsters, on the other hand, are often encouraged by their parents and other members of their society to "hit the other guy before he hits you." They are instructed to be always prepared against an attack. Lower-class boys and adolescents thus may carry knives, razors, and other weapons in their pockets so that they will be ready when the fight breaks out, as it inevitably will.

Adolescents of both social groups, of course, have observed the behavior patterns of their parents and other adults. The middle-class man who is criticized or insulted may write a letter to the editor of the newspaper, send a note or rebuttal to a magazine, or ignore the situation entirely. The lower-class man frequently will challenge his tormentor "to come out in the alley and settle the matter right now." In lower-class taverns, fights break out nearly every night. In middle-class taverns (country club and fancy hotel cocktail lounges) such brawls rarely occur.

Teachers need to understand that this basic difference in aggressive behavior exists between middle- and lower-class cultures. The lower-class boys who are fighting in and around school may not be suffering from severe personal maladjustments, but may instead be merely functioning in ways which for them are very normal. Middle-class adolescents who gossip, backbite, and make protests regarding peer behavior which they regard as hostile or obnoxious are also following the accepted pattern of their culture.

## SPEECH HABITS

Teachers are usually well aware that young people from the lower and middle classes bring widely different sets of speech habits to school with them. The lower-class adolescent will use such expressions as "I seen him do it," "He has went home," "I knowed they was coming," "He don't know that I have saw him," "The bell has rang," "I brung my lunch," "The teacher learned me," and "I set on the step while I et my sandwich." A man or youth from the lower classes often refers to his wife as "the old lady" regardless of her age.

Teachers are often disturbed by the great number of "four-letter words" that lower-class boys and girls use with abandon and in the most unlikely places. Teachers, however, often fail to realize that the youngsters have, since infancy, heard these expressions used by their mothers, fathers, relatives, and playmates. One of the quickest ways to identify the social class of a person is to talk with him for two or three minutes. In that time the speech habits of his subculture will inevitably come to the fore. Young people who are making the transition from the lower class to the middle class will only occasionally make a slip that will indicate their backgrounds.

A large part of the remedial English work in our secondary schools is designed to help lower-class adolescents acquire the speech habits of the middle class. There is much more that they need to learn in order to move up the social ladder, but this is one of the major requirements.

### SEXUAL BEHAVIOR

Perhaps in no area of behavior is there a sharper distinction between the values, attitudes, and actions of adolescents from lower-class and middle-class homes than in that area referred to as sexual. "Petting," "necking," and "kissing" are largely middle-class phenomena. Adolescent middle-class girls sometimes write letters to the advice columns of newspapers complaining that their boy friends have not as yet kissed them. The girls may ask what is wrong with them or what is wrong with the boys. Usually the girls are advised to make themselves interesting and attractive and are given other hints to help make them kissable. Today, many middle-class parents would be worried if their high school daughters had never been kissed. This type of behavior is considered to be a "development task" of youth. It is a normal phase of growing up. Middle-class parents and middle-class society in general, however, frown upon direct sexual behavior among adolescents and hope that their daughters will be virgins at the time of marriage.

Quite a different attitude prevails in the lower class. Kissing and petting are sometimes viewed as being silly or even perverse. A much more direct approach to sex is made. Many a lower-class man has never kissed his wife or sex partner. A lower-class boy of fourteen or fifteen who has not had complete "sexual experience" is a rarity. One lower-class boss of a crew of workers chided a sixteen-year-old boy with the statement, "What are you saving it for—the worms?" Lower-class girls quite naturally drift into "sexual experiences" as did their mothers and older sisters.

The attitude of many lower-class parents toward adolescent sexual behavior is revealed in the following incident. Mr. Smith, the probation officer of a midwestern city, was invited to address a class at the university on his experiences among lower-class youth. He described a case which had just come to his attention.

I have spent most of the day visiting two families in the X neighborhood. The boy, George (age 15), from one family, and the girl, Isabel (age 14), from the other, have been caught repeatedly having "sexual relationships" in Lake View Park (a middle-class park). I decided to get the parents to help me solve the problem. But I received no cooperation from them. At one of the houses I was pushed off the porch and told to mind my own business. At the other I was told that "kids will be kids" and why was I "snooping around." At this point I lost my temper, pounded the table, and said, "O.K., but by golly they have got to stay out of Lake View Park. Case closed."

In the lower classes, young people quite often start families of their own without benefit of a marriage license or ceremony. Sometimes a mate will be dropped and another one taken on with little or no fuss being made. Certainly there will be no divorce, because there was no marriage in the first place. Children will be born and reared. Sometimes children will be confused as to their last names. One school principal told of a sixth-grade boy who left his last name blank on the school forms. The boy said that he was not sure of his father's name, but that he would ask his mother. The mother came to school and expressed deep regret that she also wasn't certain as to the boy's last name. She showed no embarrassment, but was exasperated that she couldn't be of more help.

## OTHER DIFFERENCES

There is virtually no end to the list of ways in which the middle-class and lower-class mores differ. For example, procedures for eating are not at all the same. In middle-class society the evening meal is a somewhat formal occasion. An effort is made to get all the members of the family to the table before activities begin. Then, in many families, someone is asked to say "grace."

Food must be passed to others before one helps himself. Exact techniques of eating, such as the placing of the knife on the plate and the use of the fork and spoon, must be followed. If one finishes before the rest, he must ask to be excused and the excuse must be granted. In lower-class homes no such formality is followed. The youngsters march out to the kitchen, pull something out of the pot, and in good weather go out on the back steps to eat. If a member of the family is late to supper, he may get nothing at all. A high school football coach of the author's acquaintance had to provide one of the players on his team, a lower-class boy, with a meal each evening during the season, because practices prevented the boy from getting home in time to compete with the others.

There are differences in the churches attended by middle-class and lower-class youth (when they attend). Some churches and gospel tabernacles accept those from the lower class with open arms; other churches cater almost exclusively to the upper or middle class.

There are cliques around school that will admit no one from the lower classes. Other cliques or gangs will be formed that contain no one but lower-class adolescents. Girls from the middle class are very hesitant to accept dates with boys from the lower class. Middle-class boys will frequently date lower-class girls secretly, but will not bring them to the school prom.

It has been reported (Hollingshead, *Elmtown's Youth*) that school teachers and administrators sometimes give deferential treatment to young people coming from the various social classes. For example, when Boney, a lower-class boy, was tardy, he was treated roughly by the principal and superintendent of schools. He was hit three times on the back of the neck and shoved outside the building. Boney never returned to high school. On the other hand, when Frank Stone, Jr. (a boy from the upper classes) was tardy, he was given the greatest of consideration. The superintendent made the following remarks on the Frank Stone, Jr., episode.

I did not want to put Frank in the detention room with the rest of the kids; so I sat him there in the outer office, and I deliberately worked around in my office until five-thirty. Then I came out and said,

"Frank, I guess you have been here long enough. You go on home and let's not have any hard feelings." I talked to his father later about the whole thing, and I think we have come to an understanding.[1]

## Race and Social Class

What many people regard as racial behavior is in many cases only social-class behavior. Uninformed and ignorant whites, for example, often state that Negroes are dirty, carry knives, don't paint their houses, or grow grass in their yards. This description, of course, fits many Negroes—lower-class Negroes. The same behavior is also typical of lower-class whites. In Negro society the class pattern is similar to that of white society. Middle-class Negroes paint their houses, pick crabgrass out of their lawns, scrub their floors, attend the opera, do not carry knives, and send their children to college. Socially, middle-class Negroes have nothing to do with lower-class Negroes. Middle-class Negroes do not want their teenagers to date lower-class Negroes.

One of the reasons that some people confuse "Negro behavior" with social-class behavior is because there is such a large percentage of Negroes in this country in the lower classes.

What has been said about Negroes applies to other racial and national groups in the country. Lower-class Italians behave like lower-class people. Middle-class Italians hold the values and exhibit the behavior patterns of middle-class people.

Teachers should not stereotype the behavior of adolescents on the basis of race, but should judge each pupil for what he himself is. Knowing the social class from which a pupil comes, however, will help explain why he behaves as he does.

## The School and Social Class

Although it is generally recognized that adolescents from the various social classes come to school with widely differing value

---

[1] Hollingshead, August, *Elmtown's Youth*. New York: John Wiley & Sons, 1949.

systems and ways of behaving, it is not always clear to teachers what they should do about it. Should teachers help lower-class youth make good adjustments to the lower class from which they come, or should they help them make the transition to middle-class values and standards? For example, what should be taught in the unit on sex education which is attended by both middle-class and lower-class youth? These are not easy questions to answer.

In America, the middle class is the dominant class. It makes the laws, enforces them, and controls and participates in most of the important activities of the country. Members of the lower classes are in a sense members of a minority group who frequently are discriminated against and who are prevented from realizing themselves fully in our society. Because of this and the fact that mobility from the lower class to the middle class is possible, this author takes the position that schools and teachers should teach middle-class values and behaviors to all pupils. Such a procedure will have an integrating effect on our society and will open vistas and opportunities for many underprivileged pupils. This country has traditionally been a land of opportunity —where the lower-class boy from the "sidewalks of New York" can rise to become a member of the United States Senate or attain other important social positions. Perhaps no agency is better prepared to assist this process than the American school.

## Readings for Further Study

Barker, R. G., and Wright, H. F., *Midwest and Its Children*. Evanston, Illinois: Row, Peterson & Co., 1954.

Charters, W. W., Jr., and Gage, N. L., eds., *Readings in the Social Psychology of Education*. Boston: Allyn & Bacon, 1963, pp. 3–21.

Davis, Allison, Gardner, Burleigh B., Gardner, Mary R., "The Class System of the White Caste," in Eleanor E. Maccoby, *et al.*, eds., *Readings in Social Psychology*, 3rd ed. New York: Henry Holt and Co., 1958, pp. 371–379.

Havighurst, Robert J., *et al.*, *Growing Up in River City*. New York: John Wiley & Sons, 1962.

Hollingshead, August, *Elmtown's Youth*. New York: John Wiley & Sons, 1949.

Stanley, William O., Smith, B. Othanel, Benne, Kenneth D. and Anderson, Archibald W., *Social Foundations of Education*. New York: Henry Holt and Co., 1956, Chapters 5, 7.

Stendler, Celia B., *Children of Brasstown*. Urbana, Illinois: University of Illinois Bureau of Educational Research and Service, 1949.

Warner, W. L., and Lunt, P. S., *The Status System of a Modern Community*. New Haven: Yale University Press, 1942.

# 4

# Adolescent-Adult Relationships

IF ONE WERE to list all the things an adult may do that an adolescent is not supposed to do, he would immediately gain an appreciation of the many potential causes of conflict between the two age groups. The adolescent is told not to smoke, not to drink, not to drive a car, and, if driving, not to drive fast or recklessly, not to go to his girl's house unless her parents are at home, not to go to an adult movie, not to stay out late, and, for girls, not to wear too much make-up. But he sees his parents and other adults doing most of these things, and many of the things they do that seem highly enjoyable are expressly forbidden him.

The adolescent, since he has ceased to be a child, is no longer satisfied in his drive to obtain status by identifying with his parents; yet he is denied a place in the adult world, where he might obtain the status he seeks. In this state of limbo he joins with others, forms his own group, and may even become hostile toward the social norms of adults. He can no longer entirely accept their standards, because he sees their inconsistencies. He may become secretive and prefer his own friends to his parents, who are thereby disturbed because they are not yet ready to let him go.

The basis of conflict between the adolescent and his parents (and other adults) is by no means a one-sided affair. The fresh vigor of youth is often envied by adults, who, in repressing their envy, deride the doings of the gang, its tastes and its fads—even though a few years before, their own foibles were no less imma-

28

ture. The Roaring Twenties, with its flappers, bobbed hair, Charleston, and black bottom; the "big apple" of the thirties; and the inane ditties of the forties are worthy competitors of the adenoidal "rock 'n roll" and the "twist" of the sixties.

## Patterns of Identification

Early in childhood, each individual develops identification within his family, usually with a parent of the same sex. This identification is extremely important, for through it the child is able to obtain a sense of security and importance and to learn appropriate sex and social roles. If all goes well, the adolescent, in his expanding social world, builds upon these earlier identifications and is soon able to create independent new roles for himself. Sometimes, however, the models are inadequate or lacking, and at other times the broadened social perceptions challenge previous identifications, thereby placing the adolescent in a position of conflict.

There are numerous arrangements by which a family transmits its feelings, images, and desires to its children. Likewise, there is an almost infinite number of combinations of parental personality characteristics. Each would create a somewhat different pattern of identification among the children, and each would have a different impact upon developing personality. The principle that young people seek to identify with adults who are closest to them will help to explain what may otherwise seem perplexing problems of development. Let us take three distinct types of parents and see how their characteristics may affect, through identification, the adolescents of the family:

1. harsh and autocratic father, gentle and submissive mother
2. gentle and submissive father, harsh and autocratic mother
3. harsh and autocratic father, harsh and autocratic mother

In number one above, a boy may identify with the father and imitate his domineering ways as a child, inhibiting or repressing any hostility he has toward his father until later, when he attempts to attain his independence by using the same aggressive patterns and basic hostilities toward other people, especially those in authority, that he has learned from his father. He can ally himself with his mother as a child, but as he grows into adolescence this identification cannot be continued, or if it is, he may develop feminine points of view and behaviors that make his social acceptance very difficult. The girl in the type-one family will likely identify with the mother, and perhaps do so with little difficulty. In adolescence, however, her seeking for independence may result in difficulties, conflicts with her father, and in extreme cases her rejection of the mores and values of her home.

In type two above, a girl cannot easily identify with her austere mother. Her rejection of a harsh and perhaps domineering mother, as well as the fact that the mother's role is inconsistent with expectations of society, makes it difficult for the girl to find a suitable role for herself. She may, however—like the boy in type one—find no other way than to imitate the model given her by her mother and become domineering in her relationships with others, especially with the opposite sex. The boy in type two may easily identify with his father, but as he grows into adolescence, he may find some difficulties as he is "pushed" by his mother. He may also find it difficult to play the proper masculine role in his relations with the opposite sex.

In the third type, there is no easy identification for either the boy or the girl. The models of behavior are restricted to the point where the child, if he identifies, must choose modes of behavior that offer him little chance of peer-group acceptance. If he is rejected at home by both parents, and if the models of behavior that are given him stand in the way of his attaining acceptance from his age group or other adults, he has little chance to develop ties with anyone.

## The Struggle for Independence and Maturity

If one were to choose any one characteristic of growth that typifies the adolescent period, it would be the search for volitional independence that will hopefully lead to maturity—to the capacity to face adequately the tasks of adult life. In some cultures, the attainment of adulthood and its responsibilities come about simply and easily. In ours it does not. Indications of immaturity among adults abound in the Western world. Job turnover, alcoholism and drug addiction, divorce, desertion of children—indeed, the major social problems of our day, while of complex origin, certainly in large measure reflect lack of successful attainment of maturity. Longer periods of schooling, child-labor laws, the unavailability of jobs for young or unskilled adolescents, and restrictive ages for marriage and voting all conspire to make the struggle for independence more difficult. Moreover, when parents do begin to relinquish control, they are likely to do so without first having given their children practice in assuming responsibility. The resulting difficulties create conflicts, and may even cause the removal of emotional support at a time when it is still sorely needed.

The areas in which the adolescent must continue to develop if he is to attain maturity and independence,[1] and which may be used as criteria of maturity for those who work with youth, are the following:

1. *Physical Maturation.* Generally there are not too many cases of adolescents being immature biologically and mature socially. Biological development in our culture is usually completed long before psychological maturity is attained. In fact, *this* is one of the problems of adolescence. As noted earlier, however, differences in rates of growth may make the young person very sensitive, and may indirectly foster, or at least influence, his later lack of psychological maturity.

2. *Controls and Inhibition.* Adulthood requires the capacity to tolerate frustrations, to accept delays, and to control one's compulsive and pleasure-seeking urges. These attainments are clearly a matter of degree, as many adults never acquire these capacities.

3. *Responsibility for One's Own Actions.* The child is not legally responsible for his actions, and except in some lower-class homes, he rarely faces his difficulties alone. In adolescence, while still legally a child, he should learn more and more to assume responsibility for what he does. Unfortunately, parents in many cases continue year after year to extricate their children from difficulties, thus preventing them from learning how to do so themselves. In middle- and upper-class neighborhoods, only a small percentage of youthful crimes ever become a matter of record. Father pays the bill, and the adolescent is let off with an admonition. High school pregnancies not consummated by marriage are "taken care of." They are clearly cases of failure to assume adult responsibilities.

[1] See Chapter 1 for R. J. Havighurst's list of developmental tasks.

4. *Social Skills.* As beginning adults, adolescents must learn a whole new set of social roles. Their roles as men or women, as responsible members of a community, and as persons with social skills and graces are not play-acting but developmental tasks necessary to becoming adults.

5. *Vocational and Economic Independence.* In today's job markets there is a very low demand for unskilled labor. Without a definite skill of some kind, the adolescent is very unlikely to become independent. Even if he is able to obtain employment, he will barely earn enough to maintain himself, let alone a family. In nearly all of our large cities there are literally hundreds of thousands of young men and women who have either dropped out of high school or have completed it without learning any salable skills. Many of them must rely for their support upon their parents or upon unstable part-time or temporary work. Those who can rely on neither will have to turn to relief or to crime. In no such cases are adolescents truly acquiring economic independence.

6. *Adult Attitudes and Values.* The normal progression finds the child identifying with the values and ideals of his parents, later with the attitudes and values of his adolescent gang, and finally with the values and attitudes of the adults of his culture and his reference groups. Until he can obtain status from his own actions and beliefs and not rely solely upon the dictates of his group, he is not mature.

Few adults ever fully attain maturity in the ideal sense, as presented in the foregoing six points. But it is toward this ideal that we should strive.

## Factors Retarding Adolescent Emancipation

Prolongation of adolescence as such does not represent a serious problem. The real problem is that the forces at work in stretching out this period of life often act to retard maturity in such a way that it is never completely attained.

### RAPID OR SLOW PHYSICAL GROWTH

The way others view him has a strong effect upon the way an adolescent views himself. Both the perception of others and his self-concept depend greatly upon body image. Teachers and parents react to adolescents more on the basis of size than chronological age. An adolescent who is small or physically inept is viewed by adults and the peer group as immature, and even rapid intellectual development does not greatly alter this perception. On the other hand, the adolescent who is large for his age but still emotionally and intellectually immature is expected to act grown up and to do more than he may be capable of doing. Both types of adolescents may have difficulties in attaining maturity. The over-large adolescent, of course, may have his emancipation handed to him, but he may not be ready for it, and the problems of anxiety that ensue make his emancipation one-sided and ineffective.

The struggles of the small adolescent may lead to resentment and a generalized hostility against authority in any form. When he finally attains emancipation, he is still continually trying to prove that he is an adult to people who do not care one way or the other. The case of Henry may further illustrate this point.

As a boy, Henry was slow to mature and quite small for his age. He was treated as a little boy by his mother and held to very strict rules by an autocratic father. He was the smallest person in his class at school, even though he was intellectually superior to nearly all of them. Not only was he teased about being small, but he was "overlooked" in sex-social affairs by both the girls and boys in his classes.

Although his schoolwork remained excellent, Henry became very aggressive. He engaged in acts of daring, got into innumerable fights with younger children larger than himself, and ridiculed his teachers and other figures of authority. As a man of forty, he still quarrels with authority figures, has moved from one job to another, and has developed avocational and recreational activities more designed to prove that he is a man than to challenge his excellent intellectual ability.

## ERRONEOUS MODELS OF MATURE BEHAVIOR

Society cultivates various symbols of maturity that have little or nothing to do with its attainment. The "man's smoke," "he can hold his liquor like a man," and "be an alluring and mysterious woman with crowsfoot makeup" exemplify our tendency to associate superficial symbols with maturity. Striving desperately for emancipation and adult status, many adolescents "fall" for these jingoisms. Of course, they are not alone. Adults, too, act as if this chimerical world were the real one. The adolescent who tries to shortcut the process of growing up by engaging in such activities may find himself in further conflict with parents and with other authorities, thereby undercutting the trust that could be a firm basis for emancipation.

## LACK OF WORK EXPERIENCE

Perhaps more than any other way, the adolescent is denied primary status in our culture by lack of opportunity for work experience. Most are not able either to attain any degree of financial independence or to acquire the satisfaction that comes from responsible and productive effort. This situation is rapidly worsening. In the years just ahead, the number of older adolescents will be greatly increased. There will be nearly twice as many seventeen- and eighteen-year-olds seeking employment ten years from now as at present, and little reason to believe that jobs (especially the kind these young people can handle) will show any significant increases.

## PARENTAL MISMANAGEMENT AND FAMILY CONFLICTS

Developmental failures and stresses almost always have their origins in the home. The parental motives and attitudes that lead to conflict are summarized in the following points:

1. Parents often expect conflict with teenagers. They have been warned, through the mass media and through overgeneralization about a few "wayward" adolescents, that they must exercise great care in allowing freedom to their own children. Thus, many of the conflicts that do occur are the result of a faulty mental set, and need not occur at all.

2. Parents often disagree as to the methods of control of adolescents and in the giving of freedoms, and they are not consistent with children of the two sexes. A boy tends to be given freedom earlier, even though in actual fact he is probably less mature socially and biologically than his sister. When disagreements are apparent, the wise adolescent quickly learns to play one parent against the other in order to obtain his wishes.

3. When they allow freedom of choice and decision-making opportunities, parents may do so grudgingly and with suspicion. Even more important, they rarely give decision-making training that is commensurate with the decisions they expect their children to make. Such suspicion and lack of training inevitably induce resentment and anxiety, and lead to mistakes that might otherwise have been avoided.

4. Parents tend to project adult motives and attitudes upon the adolescent. When they know their child is parked in a car with a boy friend or girl friend, they are likely to interpret motives and behavior according

to their own adult point of view. They imagine what *they* would be doing. Thus, distortions of the meaning and significance of adolescents' behavior are common.

5. Parents dissatisfied with the way their own life has turned out may want to control the lives of their children and thus attempt to realize vicariously their own thwarted ambitions.

These mistakes, attitudes, and motives of parents are, of course, matched by equally distorted perceptions of parents and the adult world by adolescents. While the motives for conflict may go deeply into the attitudes, fears, and unconscious aspirations of parents and their teenage children, the way in which the conflicts manifest themselves can be seen in simple everyday activities in the home.

Most commonly, the conflict between parent and adolescent centers upon such things as use of make-up, personal habits of dress, hours for getting in at night, use of the car, and household chores. Having a pitched battle over what are really rather superficial indications of a more basic struggle only serves to intensify the difficulties.

The parent-adolescent relationships that most seriously hamper emancipation and the attainment of maturity are excessive overprotection, rejection, and extreme over-evaluation of the child. The adolescent who is overprotected and not allowed to form normal peer relationships, not allowed to make mistakes and learn from them, cannot easily attain independence. The adolescent who is rejected, while he does learn to fend for himself, becomes an emotional cripple who finds it extremely difficult to become a mature individual. The child whose every whim is catered to by doting parents is not prepared for the hard knocks and the struggles of the peer group.

## Implications for Education

Relationships between adolescents and adults in our culture are universally institutionalized through the family and the school. There are no other sure contacts with adults. Other institutions such as churches and employment situations provide occasional contacts. But only the school gives the adolescent frequent and close contacts with adults of both sexes and with adults who, by sanction, embody the norms and mores of the larger society. In a variety of ways the school can insure that these relationships are used to aid the process of achieving maturity.

It can first of all help in the process of emancipation from the home. The school can sponsor activities that are accepted by the home but that do not depend upon parental supervision. It can also introduce the adolescent to the adult world, perhaps even better than the home can. By providing contacts with many adults and by study, literature, athletic contests, and field trips, it can give the young person a view of the adult world that is not usually possible in the more narrow confines of the home.

The school is also in a strategic position to give students experience in assuming responsibilities, learning and practicing self-government, and planning school activities—in short, playing adult roles. It can thereby teach understanding of, and better attitudes toward, the adults with whom adolescents come in contact. Such understanding ought to improve teenagers' relationships with adults and provide better adult models for them to emulate.

Knowing how most adolescents crave to be a part of the adult world, the school can make sure that they are treated as adults. Put negatively, the adolescent should not be treated as a child. The humility and resentment created by this kind of treatment is one of the foremost impediments to adults' achieving better relationships with adolescents.

Finally, the school can be a bridge by which the adolescent is led into the affairs of his community. It can help plan work-study programs, involve the adolescent in activities of the city government, provide opportunities for the assistance of charitable social-service agencies, and allow him to manage those school functions, such as plays and athletic events, in which the community participates. More creative communities have used adolescents as assistants in adult education classes, physical therapists, hospital aides, and even as members of advisory councils for community affairs and government. In the years ahead, much more of this type of activity will be necessary.

# Readings for Further Study

Ausubel, D. P., *Theory and Problems of Adolescent Development.* New York: Grune & Stratton, 1954, Chapter 8.

Frank, L. K., "The Adolescent and the Family," *Adolescence,* Part I, 43rd Yearbook, National Society for the Study of Education, University of Chicago Press, 1944.

Kuhlen, R. G., *The Psychology of Adolescent Development.* New York: Harper and Brothers, 1952, Chapter 12.

Strang, Ruth, *The Adolescent Views Himself.* New York: McGraw-Hill, 1957, Chapter 10.

# 5

# The Adolescent and His Peer Group

Each STAGE OF LIFE brings demands for new social learnings. The infant must learn that his fundamental needs are mediated by his parents. The child learns that his status and his activities are greatly dependent upon his family and his playmates. The adolescent must learn that he can achieve status and maturity only by playing adult roles. He strives for maturity, but is still somewhat insecure; hence he needs alliance with others like himself. In the union thus formed he finds strength and the will to assert himself in the struggle for a place in the adult world.

The social learnings of adolescence, which, of course, build upon the foundation of family relationships formed during childhood, are nevertheless now beyond the direct control of adults. Rarely does an adult have complete access to the teenage group. Instead, the anxious parent, or the teacher who is somewhat suspicious of what goes on in the adolescent "gang," may find active hostility toward his attempts to penetrate or too closely scrutinize the doings of young people.

The peer group is strong and may be imperative in its demands upon its members. But it does serve an important purpose for its adolescent members. It helps them find a role for themselves. It helps them in an insecure period attain the necessary emancipation from the home, and it teaches social skills necessary for living a community life.

## Developmental Changes in Social Groups

Each culture and the various subcultures of which it is composed foster somewhat different social attitudes that operate in the development of social groups. In general, however, there are some highly predictable changes in groups as children progress through school.

In the preschool period, children of both sexes play together in small groups (two or three children to a group). Much of the play and activity in these groups is quite egocentric in nature; that is, children play side by side, each with his own toys. Even their conversation may be directed to no one in particular. Frequently their only contact is when one encroaches upon the "territory" of another. In the early school years the groups remain quite small, but a pronounced difference in sex emerges; the boys are preoccupied with their own small groups in rough-and-tumble play, and the girls in vigorous but less combative activities. The indiscriminate acceptance of each sex by members of the other which occurred in early life may be replaced by rejection of members of the other sex as children enter middle childhood. Shortly before pubescence, and for a period of about two years thereafter, the spontaneous social groups are almost entirely unisexual. The informal grouping in school somewhat overrides this tendency, but nevertheless, on sociometric testing it is not uncommon to find in the fifth or sixth grade that not a single boy has chosen a girl on any of the social or work categories that are used.

Throughout the period of childhood, and continuing on through adolescence, the peer group enlarges in size. From the initial two or three members it often grows to as many as a dozen rather close friends. While the unisexual nature of the group persists to a considerable extent, there is now an obvious crossing of the line. There are parties and dances and school functions in which boys and girls of a given "clique" are seen together. Almost all children find a group to which they can belong. Those who do not are usually unhappy, oversensitive, and defensive about their lack of social acceptance.

## Social Acceptance—Sources and Related Factors

Much of the social life of the adolescent depends upon the opportunities provided by social and cultural agencies of his community and schools. Very frequently, barriers to social activities are erected by community attitudes, by the school, and by perceptions (sometimes distorted) that grow in the adolescent's mind. Often in high schools and even in junior high schools, activities are so conducted that many pupils feel left out. In a typical school nearly half the adolescents take part in no extracurricular activities. The majority of the socially important doings of the school may be controlled by a handful of pupils in that school.

The social life of the adolescent, of course, does *not* depend wholly upon school activities. He may take part in the downtown teen club or the YMCA. Many friendships are formed in work situations or in hobby groups outside the school. But it surely must be clear that the "social swim" is controlled by the school, and that many adolescents are on the outside looking in. They are *not* a part of the group that "counts," and they know it.

A few months ago the author chaperoned a week-end party at a city park where adolescents have a "den" at which they dance, listen to records, and play games. Even though this was a community-sponsored affair, presumably for all children, there were obvious absentees. First of all, there were no Negro children, even though the school from which the pupils came contained about 20 per cent Negro children. Secondly, there were practically no children from lower socio-economic classes. In the middle of the evening three boys, whose dress and appearance indicated that they probably were from underprivileged homes, did put in an appearance. But they were completely isolated. No one spoke to them. They were not deliberately snubbed; they were just ignored. The third notable group of absentees were the young teenagers who were immature physically or socially. What were these "unwanted" ones doing that Saturday night?

What leads to rejection, lack of acceptance, and loneliness? The study of sociometric tests, interviews, and clinical observations points to the following factors as being associated with lack of acceptance.

## SHYNESS AND WITHDRAWAL

Real or fancied deviation from the norm may lead to a variety of adjustive reactions. Sometimes the adolescent who perceives himself as different becomes defiant and aggressive.

Other adolescents may adopt bizarre forms of behavior in a bid for attention and for a unique place in the group; better to be the clown than not to be in the group at all. Still others retreat from social contacts to find solace in fantasy or in association with one or two others who are peripheral to the social mainstream. Why do some and not others make this particular reaction?

An adolescent may develop undue shyness first because the family pattern is one in which one of the parents is an egocentric with whom the adolescent is unable to compete. A second cause might be too much pressure from parents, so that the child feels that nothing he does is right. Such overexpectations produce anxiety as the adolescent tries to please but always sees himself as second-best to his siblings and peers. He may also feel that he is valued not for himself as a person but for what he can accomplish. These are the antecedents of the shy and withdrawn individual.

## SOCIAL INEPTNESS

Some adolescents are rejected not because they have deep-seated ego deficits, but because they have never learned the social skills that provide access to a group. Sometimes there is a conflict of values between home and the school group—for example, the values of certain religious sects which conflict with school activities. Often a child has been overprotected and kept from situations in which social skills can be learned. These adolescents may be particularly affected in developing social relations with the opposite sex. Undoubtedly, many tragic marriages result from just such social ineptitude. Social acceptance requires certain perceptual skills and a control of hedonistic (pleasure-seeking) impulses. These young people may have neither. Unless their deficits are corrected and skills learned, they may become pathologically shy and develop emotional difficulties.

## EMOTIONAL INSTABILITY

Young adolescents are quick to detect aberrations in personality among their peers, and are as quick to reject such differences. Whereas the child who is shy or withdrawn is likely to be simply neglected (sociometrically, he receives no votes), the unstable one may be actively rejected by the group. The following is a case which illustrates the unhappy consequences of both social ineptness and emotional instability.

Madelaine is an only child of foreign-born parents. She was hospitalized when she was four for nearly a year as a result of rheumatic fever. Much of that time was spent in a hospital some distance from her home. When she returned home, her doting parents indulged her every wish to the best of their ability, but in school things were different. Her mannerisms and lack of social *savoir faire* with her age mates developed into their active rejection of her. To counter this, she resorted to various attention-getting devices, such as eating dog biscuits and exclaiming how good they were. This, of course, only made matters worse. Even the few girls with whom she had played now deserted her. As a young adolescent, for a time she was able to find some comfort in playing with younger girls, but their older brothers and sisters (and even parents) ridiculed her so that even this avenue was closed. Finally, as a freshman in high school she found that her good looks attracted attention from older boys. She quickly capitalized upon this asset and began secretly dating college students when she was only a sophomore in high school. She "ran off" with a young man on a trip of a couple of thousand miles. Fortunately, throughout her difficulties she had the genuine affection of her parents and careful consideration of high school counselors, so that she is now somewhat accepted by her classmates. Her case is not unusual. Had it been further complicated by rejecting parents, it might have resulted in emotional habits that would probably have led to mental illness or a sociopathic personality.

## STATION IN LIFE

The stigma in our culture of belonging to certain ethnic or social groups cannot be overlooked as a contributing factor to social rejection. Various studies have shown that early in adolescence "social distance" already begun in childhood now increases greatly. The effect on the adolescent thus rejected is damaging to him and, indirectly, to all of society. Particularly affected are the Negro children, who are readily identifiable from an ethnic standpoint and who for the most part belong to the lower socio-economic classes.

## Enhancing Social Acceptance

Many of the critics of education have censured, almost to the point of abuse, teachers' efforts toward better personal and social adjustment of their pupils. These criticisms generally involve one or more of the following points: (a) The school's domain is intellectual, not affective, and teachers should therefore *not* spend time on such nonessentials as social skills. (b) The school joins with a dangerous trend in society toward conformity; social adjustment is seen as killing individuality and creative genius. (c) The family and other agencies of society, such as the church, are the appropriate avenues for social learnings. (d) School personnel are not trained to deal with such problems and should therefore *not* become involved; instead, they should refer such problems to trained personnel. Whatever the merits of these arguments (this author feels that there are very few), the fact is that the school is involved in these matters whether it likes it or not. Every junior-high-school or secondary-school teacher knows that the adolescent with whom he works brings to the classroom not just an intellect but also a personality that influences both his own learning and that of others in the class. Attitudes, values, and motives are as important in determining the outcomes of education as is intellect. In one sense they are a part of the intellect. The school that fails to consider social learning loses an excellent opportunity to exert a healthy, positive influence upon social development.

### SCHOOL-RELATED GROUP ACTIVITIES

There are dozens of opportunities in any classroom for group work of some kind to augment the individual activities associated with recitation and study. Laboratory work, school projects, field trips, drama, debates, and the school newspaper are but a few. Added to these, of course, are the many curricular or extra-curricular activities that offer opportunities for learning social skills. There is no reason to create artificial situations to bring about social interaction. Many of the tasks and problems in school are really group tasks. It is up to the teacher to manage the involvement of all the students when such tasks arise. For some adolescents, this may mean study or observation on the part of the teacher to determine at what place and point in time they can be inducted into the group.

## TEACHING SOCIALLY SIGNIFICANT MATERIAL

The substance of many courses in school relates directly to social matters. The meaningfulness and usefulness of such material may be enhanced by bringing it to bear upon the immediate local situation in which adolescents find themselves. Classes dealing with such topics as health, family living, civics and history, and literature must certainly treat material that has applicational value in greater self and group understanding. How can an adolescent learn about Alexander Pope's handicaps, his style of writing, and his amatory activities without better understanding the handicapped people he knows—or his own handicaps, for that matter? Many of an adolescent's concerns center about his home social problems. The way in which adolescents state their problems is adequate testimony of their naïveté regarding social matters. Real sophistication obviously must wait upon further social experience, but certainly the gross misconceptions that children have about themselves and about others in their group could be eliminated by a program with this end in view.

## COUNSELING

The truly inept or disturbed adolescent who is ignored or rejected by his group needs help beyond what the ordinary classroom teacher is likely to be able to provide. The modern high school ideally has one counselor for every three hundred students. Assuming that the counselor can spend half his time with disturbed students of this type and that 10 per cent of the students need such help, he will have thirty students, with whom he must work regularly. Any of the other 270 students who need help must rely upon their teachers, class advisers, deans, or their peers. Neither counselors nor teachers can change the group. What they can do is to try to change the individual's perception of himself and of the group, and thus hopefully alter his behavior so that acceptance and social skills are acquired. A clear sociometric diagnosis as well as a study of the cliques, clubs, and extracurricular groups will aid both teacher and counselor in this task.

## SCHOOL POLICY

The policy of the school can be such that it encourages social interaction and social learning and attempts to work with adolescent groups, or it can be just the opposite in each respect. Over the past quarter-century, schools have unquestionably moved toward the former position, and it would be rare to find a public high school of any size today that had not made provisions for some sort of group activities and school-related social affairs.

# Working with the Adolescent Group

Access to individual adolescents, to their problems and aspirations, is best obtained through the group to which the adolescent belongs. In fact, it may be the *only* access for the adult who wishes to bring about any radical change in values and attitudes or group structure. Instead of trying to break up gangs and cliques, successful social workers, psychologists, and teachers have managed to use these existing groups for constructive purposes, and to use natural young leaders rather than attempt to appoint new ones who satisfy the teacher but who may be not at all acceptable to the group. Like all other prescriptive formulas, however, this one has exceptions and may be very difficult to manage. As noted earlier, the adult may find antagonistic responses to his attempts to work with a group. Some gangs have good reason to be suspicious of a well-meaning adult, whom they may perceive as just one more authority figure offering little and demanding a great deal. The encouraging note here is that very often those individuals and groups that are the most openly hostile and suspicious are the very ones who most need, and eventually depend upon, the adult who works with them.

Good counseling procedures for establishing rapport and a working relationship seem equally appropriate in dealing with groups. Likewise, the general principles of social psychology, as they apply to other groups, apply as well to the teenage gang. This brief section cannot attempt to provide the complete background that may be obtained in these basic disciplines, but some generally recognized avenues for dealing with groups of young people are presented in the following sections.

## SIGNIFICANT ACTIVITIES

Everyone wants to feel a sense of competence and significance. The adolescent, particularly, operating as he is from a position of insecurity, craves to take part in activities that have an important bearing upon the affairs of the day. He will picket, get signatures on petitions, distribute baskets to the poor, or make a door-to-door survey of his neighborhood, if he is convinced that such things are significant. It should be remembered that during the last war some of the most vigorous resistance fighters in the Scandinavian countries and in Yugoslavia were school-age boys. Teachers and social workers need (1) the creative imagination to devise activities in and out of school that mobilize the energies of the group for such constructive purposes and (2) cooperation from the community in making funds, services, and facilities available so as to capitalize upon these compelling urges.

## BUILDING RAPPORT

There is no simple rule that can be applied in building a relationship with people, especially when they are already in an organized group with values and attitudes contrary to the very thing being attempted. Those who have been successful suggest the following: (1) make the ground rules of the relationship clear—that is, indicate such things as the extent to which volitional choice is open; (2) be accepting of the individual, even though not of his behavior—make him know that he is valued as an individual; (3) when confronted with hostility or resistance, do not push too hard or too rapidly to set up a relationship; (4) prove that you are honest, fair, and predictable. In working with adolescent groups, it is also helpful if the individual has something to offer—some obviously admired or valuable skill, some useful or stimulating goals or ideas, or some admitted need with which the groups can help. Above all, let part, if not most, of the initiative for the relationship come from the group itself. This, of course, is not always possible, but it makes for more rapid rapport when it happens.

## DEVELOPING EXEMPLARS

A great deal of the success of the Higher Horizons program in New York City springs from the fact that the Puerto Rican and Negro adolescents involved were shown for the first time in their lives other Puerto Ricans and Negroes who were working as scientists, businessmen, artists, lawyers, and athletes. These successful men and women met with the culturally deprived students, talked with them, and helped to create new kinds of aspirations for them. Consequently, school counselors and teachers were better able to gain real access to the children's thoughts and feelings and to play a constructive part in their peer groups.

## CULTIVATING DESIRABLE PERSONAL QUALITIES

Students' perceptions of their teachers determine to a great extent the social climate of the classroom. Adolescents list cooperativeness, considerateness, and patience as most important qualities for a teacher to have. They will give group access to teachers who are fair and supportive and who have a sense of humor. The rigid, irritable, and unpredictable adult, no matter how effective he is as a purveyor of subject matter, will *not* be accepted by the group, and will likely have little effect upon improving the social relations of the group. In short, he will not know his students, because they will not reveal their real feelings to him.

A cardinal principle in dealing with adolescents is that the adult avoid ego-defensive behavior. When a teacher builds his own feeling of importance at the expense of students, he destroys self-confidence, creates anxiety, and practically assures that he will be shut out by the group. On the other hand, adolescents are very perceptive of the teacher's attempts to be ego-supportive for the individual student and the group. Allowing one adolescent to "save face" can dramatically improve the atmosphere in a classroom.

## Readings for Further Study

Cunningham, Ruth, and Associates, *Understanding Group Behavior of Boys and Girls,* New York: Bureau of Publications, Teachers College, Columbia University, 1951.

Kuhlen, R. G., *The Psychology of Adolescent Development.* New York, Harper and Brothers, 1952, Chapter 7.

Strang, Ruth, *The Adolescent Views Himself.* New York: McGraw-Hill Co., 1957, Chapter 8.

Tyron, Caroline M., "The Adolescent Peer Culture," in *Adolescence,* Part I, 43rd Yearbook, National Society for the Study of Education, University of Chicago Press, 1944.

Whyte, W. F., *Street Corner Society.* Chicago: University of Chicago Press, 1943.

# 6

# Physical Development

IN MANY RESPECTS, human development is a continuous process from conception to death, various aspects of development being closely determined by what has gone before. Moreover, many of the problems of development apply to one age of life as well as to another. However, the beginning of adolescence, known as pubescence, brings with it abrupt and psychologically significant physical changes that mark this period off from other stages of growth.

While many of these important physical changes, such as growth in height and deepening of the voice, are obvious and commonly known, others are hidden or less obvious but nonetheless significant.

## Surge in Growth

Toward the end of childhood, girls at about ten or eleven and boys at about twelve or thirteen begin a period of rapid growth in height and weight (general bodily growth). This acceleration of growth is closely linked to the increased hormonal output of the pituitary gland, which serves not only as the catalyst to produce growth but also as the controller of other glands (adrenals, gonads, and thyroids) that determine both tissue growth and function. The rapid growth thus set off is maintained for a period of about three or four years, with the greatest increment in growth coming at an average age of 12.6 for girls and 14.8 for boys. During this period it is not uncommon for a child to grow as much as six to eight inches in height and to gain forty to fifty pounds in a year's time.

For a variety of reasons, physical development in this period of rapid change is characterized by asynchronies that bring concern to adolescents and their parents and teachers. Skeletal and muscular development is more rapid than the learning required to make use of the new muscle mass. Motor habits that once served the child (such as gracefully falling to the floor in play) are no longer appropriate. The new body requires new learnings. Bodily proportions also undergo changes. Facial features alter, because the growth of the lower part of the face lags behind the growth of the upper part. Legs, proportionally, usually grow more rapidly than the body stem, and hands and feet anticipate by several years the total body size of their owners.

General bodily growth is paralleled by physiological changes such as cardiovascular and respiratory growth and changes in metabolism and in general movement toward the adult status. As will later be shown, these internal changes also have manifestations and initial irregularities that may become sources of concern for the young person and his parents.

## Puberty and Primary and Secondary Sex Characteristics

Following closely on the heels of accelerated growth, the pituitary gland directs the adrenal cortex and the gonads into more activity. Prior to this time, virtually equal amounts of androgenic (male) and estrogenic (female) hormones are produced for both sexes by the adrenal cortex on direction of the anterior pituitary gland. Now an increased amount of hormonal production differentiates the sexes; the males producing more androgens, the females more estrogens. Moreover, the genital and sex-appropriate tissues become more sensitive to catalytic action of these sex-specific hormones. The dawn of these changes is reflected in girls by the beginning of the enlargement of breasts and in boys by an enlargement of the testes. There follows in each sex a series of physical changes whose appearance is highly predictable and whose sequence is unalterable. In girls the enlargement of breasts is followed by the pubic hair (first straight, then kinky), the menarche, and axillary hair.

In boys, after the initial enlargement of the testes, there occurs pubic hair, axillary hair, voice changes, and beard in that order.

Thus, by observing adolescents, it is fairly easy to determine the point in pubescence that they have reached. The observable secondary sex characteristics, such as development of axillary hair and voice change, while reliable clues, are as their term implies—secondary to the primary sex changes. Primary sex characteristics include reproductive organs whose maturity is signaled by the menarche in the girl and by the first ejaculation in the boy. The menarche, to which society probably attaches undue importance, does not indicate reproductive capacity, as it is usually followed by a year to two of sterility. In any case, society attaches significance to the first menstrual period, even though it is but one event in the total move toward maturity.

Just as the age at which the physical growth spurt begins varies greatly among individuals, so do the changes associated with pubescence. While the average age of menarche today is about thirteen years, the normal range is from nine to eighteen. Boys who mature about two years later show the same sort of range in the age at which they reach puberty. (The psychological significance of these normal variations, and of the difference in age at which boys and girls reach maturity, will be discussed in subsequent chapters.)

## Strength, Skill, and Fitness

Physical development viewed only in terms of increases in size, body features, and secondary sex characteristics presents only the gross picture of the many physical changes that occur in adolescence. Even more significant, perhaps, are the growth patterns of strength and skill, which so clearly differentiate the adolescent from his recent childhood.

The post-pubescent boy, even though he may be the same

chronological age as friends who have not yet entered pubescence, will almost certainly be stronger and will likely have greater agility, motor coordination, and bodily skills. He will, of course, rapidly overtake girls, whose strength already has increased about a year earlier and who briefly challenged him. What forces account for this development? First, it is clear that the accelerated production of male hormones (androgens) brings with it added muscular strength. Second, the nature of skeletal growth, increased shoulder breadth, larger chest cavity, and finally, the greater lung size, heart size, and increased blood pressure are all favorable conditions for physical strength. While many of these same changes are occurring among girls, their physical strength increases at a slower rate, and, of course, never equals that of males in our culture. There are two reasons for this superiority: (1) biologically, the male is favored by larger shoulder breadth, a bigger chest cavity, and better leg leverage; (2) culturally, girls receive little encouragement for the development of strength. In fact, they are encouraged in the opposite direction—to be weak and dependent, or at least to pretend that they are.

Along with increases in strength come the development of motor coordination, reaction speed, and perceptual-motor skills. For example, simple tests have been used to compare the eight-year-old, who can tap with his finger 130 times in thirty seconds, with the average eighteen-year-old, who can tap about 210 times in the same period. Reaction time, a measure of the time between a signal and a response to it, is usually reduced as much as one-third between the ages of eight and sixteen. There are, of course, great diversities among children of the same age and even of the same maturational age.

In an appraisal of physical development, one important consideration has to do with what is optimal. We speak of fat, healthy babies, but we cannot use these two adjectives together to describe any other time of life. Height-weight charts are based on the average, but may, when a large segment of youth are overweight, lead to faulty conclusions. What is average is certainly not necessarily optimal. Combining data from both growth charts and tests of physical strength and fitness clearly reveals that today many young people are overweight.

In many respects, adolescence is the healthiest time of life. The childhood diseases are past, and the degenerative disorders of adulthood are in the future. The habits of life that have to do with continued physical vigor are, however, laid down in these formative years. The young body can take enormous abuse and bounce back. Psychologically, however, the habits of abuse, once they enchain the individual, may, unless broken, assure a less-than-optimal adult life.

## Common Misconceptions

Compared with some other areas of development—for example, mental development—physical development should be clearly marked and subject to little dispute. Unfortunately, this is not true. Misconceptions about physical development are shared by both adolescents and their parents.

### AWKWARDNESS IS NOT UNIVERSAL

Adults expect adolescents to be clumsy, and to some extent they dismiss as adolescent awkwardness many difficulties for which a better explanation exists. Actually, even though there are asynchronics (as previously noted), and even though muscle mass tends to precede function, the adolescent can quickly and easily learn skills and controls. The grace of high school basketball players, cheer leaders, and young swimmers and divers makes "pot-bellied" parents awkward by contrast. In fact, one wonders if some of the adult criticism of adolescents is not partly due to the envy of the older generation, who see their own youth slipping away but are reluctant to accord children the place of prominence to which their youthful vigor, skill, and speed entitle them.

### WARM CLIMATES DO NOT ACCELERATE MATURITY

There is evidence that occurrence of puberty is more closely allied to other conditions of life, such as diet and health, than to climate. In fact, if climate does have any effect at all, it is likely that a temperate climate promotes an earlier maturity than do either a tropical or arctic climate. It is also unlikely that ethnic factors have much bearing, although, of course, genetic factors do. Early maturity is family-related.

## VIGOROUS EXERCISE DOES NOT DAMAGE THE HEART

Growing children need physical exercise just as they need food and rest. There are important cardiovascular changes in adolescence. The heart increases in size and strength, and blood pressure increases. These observations have led some to believe that in late childhood and early adolescence vigorous exercise may be harmful. There is little evidence that this is so. As a matter of fact, this author knows a boy who had an organic defect of a heart valve. He engaged in normal physical activity, including Little League baseball, upon a doctor's advice. Eventually, in his fourteenth year an operation restored the heart to normal functioning. The point is that he suffered no heart damage, even though his heart allowed for handling only a fraction of the amount of blood handled by a normal heart. (This example should *not* be construed to mean that vigorous activity is good for everyone. For some pathological conditions, exercise is not advisable.)

## A STRONG BACK DOES NOT MEAN A WEAK MIND

Undoubtedly some adolescents who do poorly in academic work may compensate by developing physical strength. However, all studies relating mental ability to physical development show, if anything, a slight positive correlation between such ability and both size and strength. The exceptional cases are, of course, vivid.

## ACADEMICALLY ABLE YOUTH ARE NOT MOTOR MORONS

The sedentary pursuits of the bright child may remove him from the normal game learnings that most children acquire. He may consequently appear inept. However, given an opportunity for practice, he will develop game skills as well as, or better than, his less-bright peer. The point is, of course, that he may not want to. He may never learn to dig a hole with a shovel, sweep with a broom, bat a ball, or use a screwdriver, and, if called upon to do these things, he will indeed appear awkward. Whether *all* adolescents should learn some of these more common skills is a moot question.

## PHYSICAL SIZE IS NOT A GOOD MEASURE OF MATURITY

A serious error made by both parents and teachers is that physical size (height and weight) are indicators of maturity. While there is a relationship, it is so slight that little value can be placed upon it. Expecting too much of a large, immature adolescent can give him anxieties and feelings of inferiority, while treating a mature but small adolescent as a child can build resentment and aggression.

## OTHER MISCONCEPTIONS

There is a host of other misconceptions related to secondary sex characteristics and appearances. The notions that excessive hairiness denotes masculinity in women, that broad hips in boys indicates feminity, and that a low forehead points to low intelligence are but a few of the nonsensical ideas that may still exist. The school should treat them as sheer nonsense, thereby relieving the anxiety of the adolescent who possesses these characteristics.

## Special Implications for Education

All teachers, not just coaches and counselors, engage in exchanges with adolescents that involve both their physical and mental attributes. Especially at this period of life, physical appearance, rapid physical change, and preoccupation with the body and its processes impinge upon all adolescents activities.

Following are some of the special implications for education derived from what is known about the physical development that takes place at this period of life.

1. Asynchronies in individual growth are as inevitable as the variability in rates of growth among groups of children. Out of the differences thus produced among adolescents, and the difference between the adult model and the way they perceive themselves at the moment, arise many of the sensitive reactions of adolescents to each other and to adults. These "facts of life" cannot be changed. The teacher of adolescents can only hope to provide a better understanding of the process of growth, the changes and difficulties it may bring, and a sense of values which places greatest importance upon the less tangible elements of character and personality.

2. It should be clear that in the physical realm, just as in English or mathematics, no single schedule of activities will be suitable for all children, and remedial work in physical skills is just as appropriate as it is in reading, speech, or arithmetic.

3. Strength and motor skill, particularly among boys, is significantly correlated with popularity, feelings of adequacy, and social adjustment. The small, inept boy may have to be aided to achieve a place in the group.

4. Because of the wide range of strength and skill, even between adolescents of the same size, care must be taken to assure that unfair competition between mismatched adolescents does not develop. This author remembers vividly the instance in his own schooling when a large prepubescent boy was matched in boxing against a smaller post-pubescent boy. Even though the physical-education teacher finally stopped the one-sided match, a good deal of psychological damage had already been done. Naturally, such events will occur "by themselves" on the playground or in the neighborhood where pupils live. But they certainly ought to be rare at school, where teachers who know about adolescents are directing their activities.

5. Habits of diet, exercise and recreation, sleep, work, and study not only have immediate physical impact upon the adolescent, but also (and perhaps more important) may become so firmly entrenched that they continue into adult life. Schools have shown a laudable awareness of these factors upon physical development and health by requiring courses in health and hygiene and by being concerned with the carry-over value of activities learned in physical education. By and large, however, health classes may be little more than labeling parts of the body and memorizing lists of vitamins and food elements, and physical-education classes the playing of games that will never be played again after the student leaves school. What is wanted is a program in which the students are so strongly and personally involved that they will carry into their homes and their daily routines the elements of health and fitness that they learn at school. The teacher who wishes to accomplish these aims might well consider such activities as the following:

    a. Have students make a distribution of heights and weights for several classes, then test groups for physical fitness.

    b. Get students to conduct a dental survey.

   c. Do an experiment with animals, feeding some an adequate diet and others an inadequate diet.

   d. Make reports on various kinds of common physical disorders and their relations to early life.

   e. Emphasize games and sports which (1) have carry-over values, such as golf, tennis, badminton, skating, swimming, and the like, (2) do not depend for success and enjoyment on sheer physique and strength, and (3) provide the satisfaction of improving one's ability by oneself rather than by competition with others.

# Readings for Further Study

Ausubel, D. P., *Theory and Problems of Adolescent Development.* New York: Grune & Stratton, 1954.

Knapp, C., and Jewett, A. E., eds., *The Growing Years: Adolescence.* Washington, D. C.: Yearbook, American Association for Health, Physical Education, and Recreation, 1962.

National Society for the Study of Education, *Adolescence,* Part I, 43rd Yearbook. Chicago: University of Chicago Press, 1944. Chapters by Greulich, Jones, Stolz and Stolz.

Pressey, S. L., and Kuhlen, R. G., *Psychological Development Through the Life Span.* New York: Harper and Brothers, 1957, Chapter 2.

Stolz, H. R., and Stolz, L. M., *Somatic Development in Adolescence.* New York: The Macmillan Co., 1951.

# 7

# Intellectual Development

Many of the basic components of mental development are nearly complete before the adolescent period is fairly begun. Capacities such as perceptual-motor skills, space perception, and the ability to remember show little gain beyond the period of late childhood. This is not to say that intellectual growth stops, but that the groundwork for its development is fairly well completed early in adolescence.

The environmental factors that influence intelligence as well as differences in rate of growth combine to produce wide variations in ability in adolescence. Of course, these same differences exist among adults, but adults are not generally tested, nor do they compete with each other intellectually in the same way that adolescents are forced to do in school. One result of such competition is that adolescents begin to accept their perceived ability as an unchanging trait that forever places them at a given level among their peers. They do not so clearly see, nor do their parents, that intellectual development does continue and relies heavily for its growth upon the interests and attitudes of students —in short, upon their desire to learn.

## Factors to Be Considered in Intellectual Growth

The idea of intelligence as a general, innate potential that will develop regardless of circumstances has little practical value. The mental capabilities of adolescents are a composite of many influences. By mid-adolescence, interests and abilities have become specialized, interests and motivation have blended in an inseparable way with ability, and habits of thinking, conceptual development, and the strategies used to solve problems have merged into a common pool of attributes that are all reflected by mental test scores. Even the testmakers no longer maintain that they measure potential. Rather, they call their instruments aptitude or scholastic-ability tests, which are designed for the prediction of school achievement. As a matter of fact, most of the measures used could well be described as general achievement tests.

Some of the factors of mental development that should be considered in educational and vocational planning and in teaching adolescents are given in the following sections.

## CONTINUATION OF INTELLECTUAL GROWTH

Even though many of the basic mental processes level off in adolescence, there is continued growth in measured ability or aptitude throughout this period. It is probable that more complex mental activities, such as abstract reasoning, continue to develop into the early twenties. Moreover, it is obvious that learning continues regardless of when the capacity for learning levels off. Continued intellectual sophistication, the accretion of conceptual depth and more complex cognitive structure, and the learning of new skills and methods all become part of the operating or functional intelligence.

## INCREASING SPECIALIZATION OF ABILITIES

In early childhood a test of intelligence that has several subtests or part scores will show considerable intertest variability. Nevertheless, there will tend to be a fairly high intercorrelation among all the subtests. By the same token, a child who is a good reader in the third grade is also likely to be good in arithmetic and in geography. In adolescence and continuing into adulthood, while the same generalization holds to some extent, there is much lower correlation among the subtests of an aptitude battery; in short, there seems to be a greater specialization of abilities with increasing age. The adolescent who is good in mathematics may not be at all proficient in theme writing or in social studies. Plans for acceleration or homogeneous grouping need to take account of the increasing intra-individual variation in abilities. At one time, many commonly used tests of scholastic ability yielded but a single score. It was thus difficult to know the make-up of a student's aptitudes. In the past decade, however, many major standardized tests yielded a number of scores from which a profile of abilities or achievements could be drawn. Such profiles seem to provide more useful information for counselors and advisers, as well as for the students themselves.

## DIFFICULTIES OF MEASUREMENT

Errors of measurement and of assumptions in interpreting test scores can be made concerning any age level. There are, however, some special considerations for adolescents and young adults that should be noted. First of all, mental testing starts with the assumption that the motivation is constant during the testing situation; the person must want to get the right answers. This assumption probably comes closer to being met for the more tractable young child who believes he is playing a game than for the adolescent who knows it is a test and yet may not care or even wish to do well on it. Also from a motivational standpoint, it is clear that some adolescents have suffered years of defeat in tasks of just the sort that an aptitude test requires of them. In this latter case, a low score could be as much an indication of personality difficulties as of low mental ability.

Obtaining an adequate sample of all that an adolescent's abilities and achievements include is a difficult task, especially within a reasonable amount of time allotted in testing programs. The total scope of a young child's abilities can be tapped and sampled much more easily than those of an adolescent. This problem is complicated further when attempts are made to obtain scores for six to ten sub-areas of ability. The number of items that can be used to tap each special ability can become dangerously small and hence untrustworthy indicators.

## Factors That Retard Intellectual Growth

If it is granted that much of what we label intellectual growth is a product of learning, it then appears that without proper opportunities and experiences mental growth will suffer, and so the research evidence indicates. Even when adequate growth does occur, certain vicissitudes of life may create situations that hinder the natural flourishing of intelligence. In the discussions that follow, there has been no attempt to describe or treat the nearly one hundred kinds of organic defects that may be associated with, or contribute to, mental retardation. Following are the factors, other than organic ones, that militate against intellectual growth in adolescence.

### CULTURAL DEPRIVATION

Intelligence, since it reflects learning and since its very definition is culturally determined, is inextricably linked with our civilization and its opportunities and demands.

This author once had a Nigerian student who joined a class discussion of the relationship between culture and intelligence. He turned to the student sitting next to him and said: "I have an intelligence-test item for you. What would you do if you were walking through the jungle armed only with a wooden spear, and suddenly saw a leopard in a tree above, about to spring on you?" The American student replied, "I don't know," to which the Nigerian aptly retorted, "It's too late for you to be intelligent; you're already dead." In a very real sense most of us, if placed suddenly in a jungle, would be culturally deprived as far as the demands of that way of life are concerned. By the same reasoning, many young people today are thrust into a complex world for which they have inadequate background and opportunity. Their early learnings include little in the way of abstract thinking, verbal usage of any complex nature, and all of the other things we call intelligent behavior. Consequently, they not only score low on intelligence tests, but also do poorly when faced with the technological demands of society. Children in communities isolated from the mainstream of our culture—for example, those from the hills of the Ozarks, the "Black Belt" of the Deep South, or the slums of New York or Chicago—show definitely lower scores on tests and in school achievement. Furthermore, as time goes on, their relative deficit increases, so that in adolescence they would have scores on tests lower than the average child of the intermediate grades.

## SELF-DEFEATING ATTITUDES

If lack of opportunity were the only contributor to low academic aptitude, such deficits could probably be rectified fairly well by intensified opportunities and remedial exercises in school. Because many adolescents are the victims of years of adverse influences and defeats in school tasks, negative attitudes are firmly entrenched. These adolescents have developed a poor self-image and a low aspirational level, which make it unlikely that the ordinary school program can have much impact upon them. Without proper motivation and attitude change, good mental abilities cannot develop. This problem is complicated by the fact that the early school years may find the children failing to learn basic skills such as reading and arithmetic. Thus, a circular kind of difficulty is created, in that the child who fails to read also fails to learn other things, and by the time he is in the intermediate grades he despairs of ever catching up. By the time he becomes an adolescent, it is difficult for him to accept the learning of these basic skills as the proper activity for a person of his age.

## NEGLECT AND ABUSE

Sometimes the neglect and abuse of children is so great that their intellectual development is impaired. Institutionalized children, those who are badly neglected in homes or isolated from other children or adults, and those who are cruelly and quixotically punished may be so disturbed that they not only fail to learn, but are also so emotionally beclouded that they could not function in an intellectually proper way in any case. In extremes, these children and adolescents may develop neurotic and psychotic reactions and actually be judged feeble-minded, though the more proper name would be pseudo-feeble-minded. Such children, when given a normal environment, may show dramatic improvement and develop quite normally.

## Some Misconceptions

The great preoccupation of the general public with mental measurement, the comparison of children by status-seeking parents, the unfortunate overgeneralizations made by a few poorly informed teachers, and the attacks upon testing by journalists and educational critics have resulted in confusions and misconceptions about testing and mental development.

### THE INTELLIGENCE QUOTIENT

The IQ, in late adolescence, becomes practically meaningless. As previously indicated, an adolescent's abilities have become more and more specialized, so that a single score cannot possibly describe his mental achievements. Moreover, IQ scores earned in grade school may show a coefficient of correlation of no more than .55 or .6 with such scores in adolescence. Thus, it is safe to assume that (1) a single score, such as IQ, even if it is carefully and reliably obtained, is not sufficiently descriptive for placement and guidance; (2) previous IQs are not sufficiently predictive of present ability to be reliable; (3) IQ is an inappropriate label for adolescents, particularly those in the late teens. Adolescents themselves should be brought to an appreciation of the complexity of human ability, the great differences among people in various kinds of ability, and the possibilities of development along the lines of special interests and abilities.

### RAPID AND SLOW ACHIEVERS

Rates of growth differ. Figure 2 simplifies this concept graphically. Obviously, the distance from A′ to B′, will be greater than that from A to B. In other words, Jim will in a sense be more su-

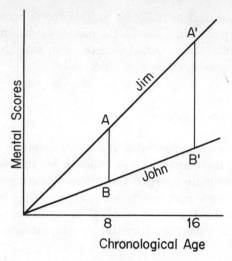

Figure 2. Increasing differences with increasing age and different growth rates.

perior to John at sixteen than he was at eight. Thus, in adolescence the differences in intellectual achievement are greater than in childhood. At one time, the slower rate of growth of children of lower ability was mistakenly assumed to be a termination of development at an earlier age. Present evidence, however, is to the contrary. Barring disease or injury, growth continues for many adolescents into their twenties and, for certain functions, probably on into their thirties and forties.

It is thus a tragic error to assume that a child of low tested ability has learned all he can learn by the time of the legal school-dropout age. An extra year or two for him could be critical, for he might finally have reached a growth point at which, for the first time, abstract learnings are possible.

## SEX DIFFERENCES IN ABILITIES

Differences in ability to learn between the sexes are probably nonexistent. The old idea that girls are poorer at reasoning or problem-solving and that their intellect is clouded by emotional and sentimental forces is nonsense. There are differences between boys and girls in various tests of aptitude and achievement; for example, tests of language ability favor girls, and those of quantification and mechanical ability favor boys. These, of course, are largely produced by differential roles assigned to boys and girls by our culture.

## INTELLIGENT ADOLESCENTS ARE NOT ODD

It is most unfortunate that the very intelligent person has so often been depicted as a maladjusted individual destined to live a sheltered and lonely life. No doubt there are such cases, but by and large the academically precocious adolescent tends to be well adjusted, socially skillful, and in no way to be pitied. Terman's famous five-volume series presenting a longitudinal analysis of "gifted" children carried through to adulthood, *Genetic Studies of Genius,* present clearly the evidence that such individuals as a group are at least as well adjusted as others.

## ETHNIC DIFFERENCES IN INTELLIGENCE

So far as present evidence indicates, there is little reason to believe that young people from one ethnic group are disposed by genetic inheritance toward any greater or less mental ability than any other. As already noted, different cultures make different kinds of demands upon mentality, and what one culture calls intelligence might be scorned as useless by another. We do know that in our country very high and very low mental-test scores are turned in by students of all ethnic and nationality groups, and any differences that have been noted can more reasonably be ascribed to the circumstances of life than to genetic differences.

## The Role of the School

The school of the future will not be content simply to administer tests of aptitude and sort out children into special sections according to their abilities. Instead, beginning early in the grades and continuing into secondary school, they will make an assessment of abilities, interests, and difficulties and plan individualized educational programs accordingly. If a child makes a low score on a test of spatial perception, they will do more than simply counsel him out of training as an architect. They will determine what is a minimal level of need for this ability in our society, and try to provide experiences that will develop it. In short, they will not simply wait for talent to emerge; they will bring it out.

## TESTING PROGRAMS

Tests of various kinds of achievement and aptitude presently exist in great numbers. Many of the leading test publishers have developed programs of standardized testing that provide a profile of achievements for the adolescent and his teacher. In some states there are state-wide testing programs sponsored by the state office of education or the state university. In either case the school should not be content to have its testing program prescribed for it, but should actively seek out the best possible group of tests for its local needs. Schools that want to select a test or a battery of them ought to (1) acquire either consultative help or use their own specially trained staff as consultants, (2) read references such as O. K. Buros' *Mental Measurements Yearbook*, as well as test manuals and other data supplied by the publisher, (3) have staff meetings at which teachers are consulted and later given information about the tests being used, and (4) give explanations to students and their parents of the kinds of tests and their purposes.

In any case, the better school will not be content with information from either the test publisher or other schools. It will conduct local studies of such matters as the predictive value of the various tests that are used, interrelations among tests, and follow-ups of students who have dropped out of school or who have gone on to employment or college after graduation.

## COUNSELING AND GUIDANCE

The professional counselor will usually acquire in his training program several courses in the use and interpretation of tests. He will be able to provide help to the teachers whose duties require them to provide advice in their day-to-day contacts with students. Obviously, the counselor cannot work with all the students in the school. Instead, he will devote his time to the most difficult problems and serve as a staff consultant for the rest of the teachers. His role demands that he be well trained in adolescent psychology and development, as well as in measurement. Some states and universities are now requiring that certified counselors obtain at least two years of education beyond a bachelor's degree.

## CURRICULAR CONSIDERATIONS

From all that has been said about the intellectual achievement of adolescents, certain implications for the school program and methods of teaching should now be apparent. The more important ones include:

1. Slow development and negative attitudes will make it essential that both the junior high school and the high school provide good remedial programs in the basic skills.

2. The extent of intra-individual variability and of the development of special abilities argues for the development of comprehensive programs and curricular offerings, so that such abilities can be properly nurtured and the adolescent can gain a feeling of significance—can take something useful from the school into society and seek further training, instead of dropping out of school as soon as possible, equipped for neither vocation nor avocation and resistant to any further learning.

3. Grouping of children on the basis of scholastic-aptitude scores will do little more than satisfy a few parents. If grouping is to be done, it should be handled on the basis of a profile of achievement tests plus other information about past performance of the student. Once grouping has been done, there should then be a real difference in the way in which groups of various levels and interests are handled; in short, curricular alterations should be made. The idea of handling *Silas Marner* slowly in one group, at an average rate of speed in another group, and rapidly in a third group is patently ridiculous. Why group adolescents at all if they are all going to read the same version of *Silas Marner,* especially since simplified editions are available?

# Readings for Further Study

Ausubel, D. P., *Theory and Problems of Adolescent Development.* New York: Grune & Stratton, 1954, Chapter 10.

Bayley, Nancy, "On the Growth of Intelligence," *American Psychologist,* Vol. 10, 1955, pp. 805–818.

Klineberg, Otto, "Negro-White Differences in Intelligence Test Performance: A New Look at an Old Problem," *American Psychologist*, Vol. 18, April, 1963, pp. 198–203.

Kuhlen, R. G., *The Psychology of Adolescent Development*. New York: Harper and Brothers, 1952, Chapter 3.

National Society for the Study of Education, *Intelligence, Its Nature and Nurture*, Part II, 39th Yearbook, 1940.

Segel, David, *Intellectual Abilities in the Adolescent Period*. Washington, D. C.: Federal Security Agency, 1948.

Terman, Lewis M., and Oden, M. N., *The Gifted Child Grows Up: 25 Years Follow-Up of Superior Groups*, Vol. IV, Genetic Studies of Genius. Stanford: Stanford University Press, 1947.

Wolfle, Dael, *America's Resources of Specialized Talent*. New York: Harper and Brothers, 1954.

# 8

# Development of Interests, Attitudes, and Values

IN EARLY LIFE the motivational, affective elements of the child's personality are in a state of flux. The healthy child has many interests, is easily led from one task to another, and with equal ease can be convinced of the rightness or wrongness of anything. It is amusing to see the child's reaction to a movie or play in which he quickly wants to identify the "good guys" and the "bad guys." He readily adopts the values and attitudes of his parents, even including the attitudes they have toward him.

The adolescent, however, does not accept at face value the dicta of either the family or the school. In fact, in his urgent striving for emancipation he may deliberately reject such values, or profess that he does, as a means of showing his independence. Moreover, he and his group have now intellectually reached a point where they can subject to a reality check the blindly accepted rules of childhood.

Unfortunately, the methods used to determine the nature of interests, attitudes, and values leaves much to be desired. Commonly, investigators have used interviews, questionnaires, opinion polls, observations, and in a few cases depth analyses. The conflicting findings of such studies lead one to suspect that we may have only a superficial view of what the attitudes and values of adolescents really are. It is also likely that there is a discrepancy beween studies because of the time at which they

were conducted; for example, studies of the relative importance
of TV in shaping attitudes and interests, conducted only a few
years apart, give quite different results. There is also a discrepancy between what adolescents say they do and what they actually do. There is not an adequate or well-accepted theory of the
way in which these aspects of the personality are developed.
There are, however, a number of well-accepted trends in development and rather clear implications for those who teach junior-
high and senior-high school pupils.

## Developmental Trends

Generalizations about the development of attitudes, ideals,
and values of adolescents are rather culturally bound and, of
course, vary from one decade to another. What interests adolescents today in Chicago might become completely passé in
another generation, and might be different from what interests
adolescents in New York or Hawaii. Moreover, the values of a
Quaker teenager in Indiana would be quite different from those
of a Jewish adolescent in Brooklyn. Nevertheless, there are certain trends of development that cut across geographical and cultural lines.

### DECREASE IN NUMBER OF INTERESTS

Young children, especially healthy and bright ones, have
many interests. They are likely to show keen curiosity about hap-
penings of all kinds in the classroom, on the playground, and
around home. With increasing age, they are interested in fewer
and fewer things, and in adolescence they may show active resistance to attempts to interest them in activities in which school
and home feel they ought to participate. This is not to say that
the energy from which interests spring decreases; it does not.
Instead, the adolescent puts more energy into fewer channels,
especially diverting much energy into those activities of a social
and heterosexual nature.

## STABILITY AND SPECIALIZATION OF INTERESTS

Measured interests of adolescents show a rather surprising amount of stability over a passage of time. The specializations begun in early adolescence in such things as athletics, literature, music, and hobbies tend to persist throughout adolescence and into adulthood. It would therefore seem that the years of late childhood and early adolescence are very important in the cultivation of significant modes of behavior and motivational habits. The present practice in many homes and schools of postponing all thought about vocations and life activities until late high school is probably a mistake, in view of these facts. The college-bound youth should begin to learn about and identify with college-type activities as early as the junior high school, and the youth who wishes to enter a trade could well begin to think about it and "role-play" it (if not get actual experience in it) at the same time. Moreover, it seems that if we wish to develop lifelong avocational interests that include such items as recreational reading, vigorous physical activities, and creative hobbies, we should begin much earlier than is now the customary practice.

## DECREASE OF INTERESTS IN SCHOOLWORK

On the average, there seems to be a decline of interest in school subject matter in adolescence. Whether this is an inevitable consequence of the narrowing and specialization of interests is not known. It is likely that the greater capacity for reality-testing, the cumulative effects of defeat in academic pursuits, the growing social and sex interests that find little outlet in schoolwork, and the perceived gap between schoolwork and vocational aspirations all may contribute to this apparent decline in interest. Certainly it is not a universal decline. Many adolescents whose schoolwork has fulfilled basic needs for accomplishment and significance, and who have been very successful in academic work, continue to view school with avid interest and look forward to a new term with eager anticipation.

## SOCIALIZATION OF VALUES

Values, especially moral ones, are accepted quite uncritically by the young child. To lie is morally wrong, and there are no exceptions. Semantically the child operates with a very highly polarized evaluative dimension (good or bad, black or white). In adolescence, values tie more to social forces. A "white lie" to save someone's feelings is accepted, and youth begin to see that there are points somewhere in between good and bad. A given kind of behavior is judged in great part by its effects upon others.

Some people believe that this kind of social morality is a poor substitute for a more dogmatic and clear-cut ethical system. Be that as it may, this trend does exist in our culture, and the realization of it is necessary in order to understand the adolescent.

## CHANGING IDENTIFICATIONS

Adolescents' broadening social and intellectual horizons lead them to identify with personalities in the remote or imaginary world, as contrasted with the child who more often identifies with real persons in his immediate environment. Also, instead of identifying with the obviously glamorous persons such as TV stars, which is characteristic of the child, the adolescent tends to relate himself to attractive and successful young adults whom he reads about or knows, and to make his ideal a composite of somewhat more abstract qualities rather than an actual person. Disquieting is the fact that the identifications of a fairly large percentage of adolescents indicate that they have aspirations that may be unrealistic for their potentialities.

## Change and Development in the Self-Concept

The onset of puberty is perceived as an abrupt change by the adolescent. In a matter of days he is expected to change the image of himself from that of a child wholly dependent upon his parents to that of a young adult. Moreover, his body, which may have been quite satisfactory in childhood, begins to change at an accelerated pace. His head and face may change in ways that are far from flattering. When he looks into a mirror, he may see a weak jaw (it will, of course, develop with time, but he may not know it), a nose larger than he likes, and a skin full of blemishes. Along with this physiognomic view, he may anxiously (albeit furtively) compare his secondary sex characteristics with peers and with adults. Few adolescents are completely satisfied with what they see.

As a child, the individual may have been accepted pretty much for what he was, and his feeling of status was largely a matter of family sanction. In adolescence, status, and consequently his self-image hinge in part on what he *has*, where he comes from—in short, upon his station in life. Furthermore, his feeling of status and importance can no longer be derived wholly through his parents. He now must seek status in a peer-group setting.

The narrative or descriptive report cards of primary school are supplanted by letter grades, and the informal games of childhood are replaced by formal recreational activities with places for only a few of his group. He either makes the team or does not. In comparing himself and his achievements with others, he is now intelligent and perceptive enough to see where he stands and to appreciate very keenly his being left out, if he is, or placed at a low rung on the social or academic ladder.

In a very real sense the adolescent internalizes all the views of himself furnished by others and by his comparison with others, and makes out of it a self-concept that may, even in mid-adolescence, become stabilized and difficult to change. In some cases the discrepancy between his perceived self and his idealized self (the way he would like to be) is so great that he despairs of ever realizing his ambitions and desires, and may give up in actually coping with the real change that he could make if his aspirations were more realistic or if his view of himself were not so deprecating.

A democratic society's ideal is to provide an opportunity for every person to develop to his full potential. Thus far, no society has approached very closely to this ideal. Social hierarchies, ethnic attitudes, religious differences, the unbridled and pathological drives for power of some individuals, and imperfect political machinery all contribute to inequities. The adolescent, in striving for a place in the larger scheme of things, may not at first see these imperfections, or if he does, he may become an idealist who sees some easy solution to all of our problems. But sooner or later he begins to gain a feeling of the insignificance of his individual efforts toward changing the injustices that he perceives. At this point he can do one of several things. He can give up and rationalize his defeat. He can identify with others and join groups whose combined voices do make a significant difference. He can struggle on, hoping to contribute a little. He can blind himself to the realities of the world. Whatever path he chooses will depend upon, as well as help determine, the kind of self-concept he develops.

## Forces That Shape Attitudes and Values

Acquired information may alter not only the adolescent's cognitive structure but also his affective make-up, his character and personality. Since adolescence is a time of transition and rapid change, the young person is groping for the meaning of the physical and social world. The philosophy of life that he is seeking comes to him from a variety of forces and sources of information —from the people and institutions that surround him.

### CULTURAL AND SOCIO-ECONOMIC LEVEL

By selective reinforcement of particular responses and by providing different kinds of models of behavior, various cultural groups and different socio-economic levels bring about different attitudes and values among adolescents. As was shown in Chapter 3, lower-class adolescents may have very different attitudes about property, violence, schooling, sex, and religion than their middle-class peers. Even family values and the concept of self are different among different cultural groups. For example, the ego development of the Negro adolescent, as well as his aspirations, motivations, and self-attitudes, are all influenced by his

membership in a lower strata of society and by his being forced
to live in a segregated, "colored" culture.

## THE MASS MEDIA

Not long ago a popular radio announcer on one of the stations
that adolescents "live with" began a campaign for cleanliness. He
suggested that at a certain hour all the teenage listeners take a
bath or shower. The results were indeed dramatic. Water pressure in the city decreased so much that the city officials were
forced to intervene. Had there been a major fire, there would
have been insufficient water to douse the blaze. Hair styles,
modes of dress, stylish fads in conversation are all greatly dependent upon the press, TV, and radio. What the teenage hero
of the moment is eating, wearing, or "recreating with" compels
attention and often emulation. Obviously, adolescents are not
unique in being so influenced, but they tend to be less critical,
more easily aroused, and, as already shown, more compelled to
conform to what other adolescents are doing.

## THE PEER GROUP AND ITS LEADERS

Recently at the Steel Pier in Atlantic City, New Jersey, where
popular bands and singers perform, a significant observation was
made. During one of the spirited demonstrations that seemed to
be touched off by the appearance on the stage of a current young
"artist," the adolescents' screaming, clapping, jumping, and cry-
ing seemed to depend upon the adolescents' observations of each
other more than upon the performer, whom many were not even
watching. They were apparently caught up in the importance of
their own emotions and were imitating one another's behavior.
The power of the group, especially its leaders, must be reckoned
as a major determinant of the attitudes and values of adolescents.

## INSTITUTIONALIZED GROUPS

The many institutions of our society add much to its plurality
of values. In a simple or more primitive group, one would expect

to find common values permeating the entire culture. There would be one religious belief, one set of conduct norms, one view about man's and woman's role, and so on. Not so in our complex society. Consider for a moment the variety of institutional groups that can influence an adolescent's attitudes. We have Boy Scouts, Demolays, Future Farmers of America, 4-H, YMCA, Youth for Christ, Young Democrats, Ku Klux Klan, American Nazi Party, Young Investors—to name but a handful of the hundreds of such groups. Adolescents may join such groups becaues of parental feelings or because they already have attitudes in common with a group. But it is to be remembered that these groups have an attitude-forming function as well. Most of the organized groups sanctioned by society have values compatible with the Judeo-Christian tradition upon which our laws and mores are based, but certainly not all of them are acceptable to the majority, and some may perpetuate beliefs that will inevitably mean personal conflict for the adolescent.

## Morality and Religious Beliefs

Contrary to a former popular impression, adolescents do not go through a period of great moral and religious upheaval. Adolescents are, of course, wise enough to see the challenges to dogma that exist through reason. They are searching for meaning and a value in life, and they are sometimes filled with an almost crusading kind of zeal to remake the world. But these high ideals do not generally conflict enough with reality to result in any major amount of religious conversion or moral upheaval. The moral, ethical, and religious trends laid down in childhood continue into adolescence and on into adulthood for most young people.

Adolescents do begin to question the systems of ethics and dogmas that they accepted at face value when they were children. Hopefully, the answers they obtain will be reasonable and consistent. Actually, they may find, as already pointed out, that there are conflicting beliefs and moral codes held by various groups. But this conflict may be more apparent than real. Most adolescents develop identifications with people whom they admire, and therefore accept their moral codes and reject those of other groups.

Most teachers would agree that we are seeking ways to make adolescents tolerant and flexible while at the same time maintaining a firmness of moral conviction. That we attain far less than our aims is so apparent on every hand in our adult society that it is not necessary to belabor the point here.

## Building and Changing Attitudes

So far as the school is concerned, the practical and urgent question is how to alter attitudes and encourage the development of ones that are acceptable to society. In the twenty or thirty largest cities of the United States, the change of attitudes and values in the large and growing slum areas may well be the most important social problem of our time. Mere attendance at school until the legal school-dropout age does not guarantee that there will be any significant alteration of attitudes and values. In fact, when our slum children enter school, they may already have attitudes adverse to those the school fosters. In adolescence, vigorous opposition and open hostility toward the values of the school are met by stringent controls and frequent expulsions which often do little more than furnish ammunition to bolster the negative attitudes that already exist. A program that is to change an adolescent's values and attitudes must involve the adolescent himself as a participant in the process. What is the school's part?

First, of course, the teacher should determine what the present attitudes are. This determination can be made with a straightforward questionnaire, interview, or, for more precise measurement, an attitude scale.

Once existing attitudes are determined, they should be brought out into the open and subjected to the scrutiny of the adolescents themselves through group discussion and perhaps by further self-analysis. Students may also profitably be encouraged to assess the community's attitudes about a particular matter and to attempt to analyze the reasons for such attitudes.

The group should then study and discuss the genesis of its attitudes and should plan for experiences that involve elements of the attitude. For example, attitudes toward labor should be analyzed by talking with labor leaders and workingmen as well as management personnel.

Some teachers have had success by planning experiences (films, stories, TV) that dramatically present the other side of a question in which attitudes are already polarized. Whatever else is done, the school must capitalize upon the great strength of the adolescent's peer group and its leaders.

## Capitalizing upon Adolescents' Interests

The enthusiasm and energy of adolescents need no description for those who have worked with young people. The excitement about such things as social affairs, automobiles, and recreational activities may seem endless. The adolescent may talk for hours with his friends about a vacation canoeing trip. Girls may plan for weeks for a dance, discussing with each other every last detail of their dress and grooming.

Unfortunately, these interests are often not at all connected with regular school activities. In the classroom John may be thinking of his chances of getting the family car, of his date that night, and of the game on Friday, and not about algebra or social studies. Through the social group, and by various logical connections, the teacher ought to be able to capitalize upon known interests.

First of all, the adolescent is interested in himself. He is preoccupied with his status, problems, and position. Work in school that gives him a feeling of significance, hence importance, will be of immediate interest. More than this, though, he needs to learn, in connection with his own self-interest, that not everything in life is going to be fun. He must realize the value of work and learn to tolerate monotony and perhaps even drudgery, when necessary. If he can relate such activities to his feeling of importance, he will have achieved a real step toward maturity. Adolescents ought to be shown that there is a real difference between the person who does something (such as schoolwork) because he is afraid not to and the one who, in his own self-interest, realizes that he must work in order to develop his abilities.

The second point is that adolescents have an awakening interest in the opposite sex. They want to engage in activities that bring them into contact with boys or girls in their class. Since much of the class activity and homework may involve problem-solving and project work, it should not be at all difficult to capitalize upon this already existing interest in furthering the learning of schoolwork.

For hundreds of years good teachers have used the existing interests of adolescents to motivate the learning of subject matter. Many principles of science do relate to automobiles, water skiing, and one's physical appearance. Literature and social studies do deal with matters that are closely related to the present concerns and interests of young people. Teachers can find the examples and demonstrations that will make this relationship apparent. If they are especially clever, they will arrange for the student to discover such relationships himself.

## Readings for Further Study

Allport, Gordon W., "Values and Our Youth," in Robert E. Grinder, ed., *Studies in Adolescence.* New York: The Macmillan Co., 1963, pp. 17–27.

Kuhlen, R. G., *The Psychology of Adolescent Development.* New York: Harper and Brothers, 1952, Chapter 9.

Pressey, S. L., and Kuhlen, R. G., *Psychological Development Through The Life Span.* New York: Harper and Brothers, 1957, Chapter 10.

Remmers, H. H., and Radler, D. H., "Teenage Attitudes," *Scientific American,* Vol. 198, June, 1958, pp. 25–29.

Strang, Ruth, *The Adolescent Views Himself.* New York: McGraw-Hill Co., 1957, Chapter 3.

# 9

# Heterosexual Development of Adolescents

ONE OF THE important tasks of adolescence is to make the transition from childhood social-sexual behavior to the new requirements of adolescence and adulthood. Before puberty, boys and girls lead quite separate lives and show only slight interest in each other's company. Following puberty, members of the opposite sex become increasingly attractive, and many new relationships and problems develop.

## Dating

Dating customs and practices are, of course, a product of the culture in which the adolescent lives. In certain oriental countries, such as Thailand, boys and girls do not date at all. They are kept separate in social functions, and it is not until the time of marriage that they are brought together by parental arrangement. In the United States dating begins, on the average, at about age fourteen for both sexes, and "going steady" at about fifteen. Many start dating and going steady much earlier. There is much controversy in the current press and anxiety among some parents because of the present practice of "going steady" at such an early age. It is believed that pairing off on a steady basis leads young adolescents into sexual and emotional intimacies long before they are ready for marriage. Anyone attending a high school dance or a dance at a teenagers' club will see fifteen-

and sixteen-year-old couples arrive together, refuse to dance with anyone but their own dates, and leave together. Having a steady date makes the adolescent feel secure and accepted by the group, which expects this kind of behavior of him. There is no reason, however, why this pattern of behavior cannot be altered, and there are, perhaps, good reasons for doing so. During the early years of adolescence a boy or girl should make many friends and have social and emotional contacts with many members of the opposite sex.

High schools which sponsor dances, for example, should arrange the evening so that a boy or girl is required and expected to exchange a great many dances. Once the school takes the lead, other agencies such as the church and community clubs should follow suit and encourage boy-girl relationships on a nonsteady basis. Boys and girls would have just as much, or more, fun and at the same time would be developing heterosexual skills and interests that are preferable to those that can be developed with a single, steady association with one member of the opposite sex. As soon as boys and girls find that this new pattern of behavior represents the thing to do, they will fall easily in line. Human nature does not suggest that there is any specified way of dating. When society decides what it wants, that is what it will get.

Dating practices have been intensively studied by Hollingshead, who reported the results in his book *Elmtown's Youth*. Who boys and girls date depends partly on the social class from which they come. The majority of dates take place between adolescents of the same social class. When cross-class dates occur, they tend to involve adolescents from an adjacent class. Adolescents in every social class except the highest also try to date persons who are a class higher than themselves in the prestige structure. Conversely, the higher-class adolescent tries to limit his contacts to adolescents who are lower than he on the socioeconomic scale. In Elmtown, Class V members (the lowest class) are so repugnant socially that adolescents in the higher classes almost entirely avoid dating ties with its members. About the only time that a date could occur between a higher-class adolescent and a Class V adolescent would be when a higher-class boy would date a Class V girl secretly for sexual purposes. Such a girl would, of course, not be invited to a school picnic, dance, or hayride.

Who an adolescent dates also depends partly on religion and whether the individual dated satisfies the social and personality needs of his partner. Dating among adolescents can serve a very useful purpose in preparing young people for marriage and adult responsibilities. The specific patterns, however, need to be studied and altered by schools and other social agencies in order that this practice may indeed fulfill its purpose.

## Necking, Petting, and Other Heterosexual Activity

Necking and petting among adolescents is not new in our culture, although such practices are probably more prevalent than in former years. Two factors partially explain the increase. First, the number of adolescents who have access to automobiles makes privacy easier to attain, and second, an opinion seems to be developing that a certain amount of sexual intimacy between young people of the opposite sexes is desirable from a mental-hygiene standpoint, and may serve as valuable experience for marriage.

Kinsey's study shows that 85 per cent of boys have engaged in petting by the time they are nineteen. Twenty-two per cent of these have "petted to climax." By the age of eighteen, 81 per cent of girls have engaged in premarital petting. Of these, 15 per cent have "petted to orgasm." Among both boys and girls, premarital petting is somewhat more prevalent among the better-educated classes of society than among those who have had meager educational opportunities.

According to Kinsey, the techniques used by adolescent boys and girls in their petting activities include simple kissing, deep kissing, breast stimulation, mouth-breast contacts, manual stimulation of female genitalia by male, manual stimulation of male genitalia by female, oral contacts with female genitalia by male, oral contacts with male genitalia by female, and genital apposition.

Many adolescents rationalize that by petting they retain their virginity and at the same time reduce emotional frustration which may lead to personality disorders. The tragedy of premarital pregnancy, of course, is avoided by petting, if the experience stops at that point. Some authorities (Terman, Kinsey) have suggested that premarital petting may actually be an aid to successful marriage. Until more convincing and valid studies are made, however, the present authors take the position that schools and sex-education programs should take a dim view of heavy petting. More personality problems are probably caused by such behavior than are eliminated. Considering the values held by present-day society, the adolescent who engages in many forms of petting runs a real risk of accumulating more guilt feelings and other social problems than he can handle. The school should play an active role in keeping adolescents so occupied with exciting curricular and extracurricular activities that premarital heavy petting will be kept to a minimum.

Kinsey's investigation further revealed that by the age of twenty, 73 per cent of boys have had premarital sexual intercourse. At this same age, only 20 per cent of girls have engaged in premarital coitus. This, of course, reflects the double standard that exists in American society. Some may wonder about the Kinsey statistics. In general, they seem to be on the conservative side. Other studies show adolescent sexual activities to exceed the percentages reported by Kinsey. This may be due partly to the fact that many of Kinsey's subjects were older people who reported their adolescent sex histories, which in many cases were probably less extensive than the activities of present-day adolescents.

As with heavy petting, premarital sexual intercourse between adolescents is not a realistic solution for the emotional problems of youth in present-day society. The sex-education programs of schools should face the problem squarely and help young people make adjustments that will be more rewarding to them in the long run and will at the same time benefit the larger social group.

## Masturbation

Although masturbation seems to be frowned upon in our society, it is almost universally practiced among healthy adolescent boys. By the age of fifteen, according to the study made by Kinsey, between 82 and 90 per cent of boys have masturbated. By the age of twenty, the range is 90 to 94 per cent, depending upon socio-economic status. Among girls the rate is considerably lower. At age fifteen only 28 per cent of girls have masturbated, and by age twenty the figure has risen to only 41 per cent. Ultimately, about 97 per cent of American males and 62 per cent of American females will have had masturbatory experiences.

What should be the attitude of the school toward this sexual practice? In the past, special lectures for boys only or for girls only were sometimes scheduled, at which a religious leader or physician would speak. The alleged evils resulting from masturbation were pointed out, but it is doubtful that these admonitions reduced the practice. In fact, such speeches may have brought the practice to the attention of some adolescents who had previously been unaware of its existence. In recent years the medical and psychological attitude seems to be that masturbation, in and of itself, is not harmful, but may instead provide some relief for pent-up sexual tension that would otherwise interfere with satisfactory schoolwork or the carrying out of other responsibilities.

The fact still remains, however, that many adolescents are in conflict about the advisability of the practice. Kinsey states that "many boys pass through a periodic succession of attempts to stop the habit, inevitable failures in those attempts, consequent periods of remorse, the making of new resolutions—and a new start on the whole cycle. It is difficult to imagine anything better calculated to do permanent damage to the personality of an individual." As for females, he states that approximately half had some psychological disturbance over their masturbatory experiences. Some were disturbed for only a single year or two, but the average female carried her anxiety for six and a half years. Kinsey believes that there is no other type of sexual activity that worries females more than masturbation.

There is no question but that the school counseling and sex-education programs should meet this problem head on. Guilt feelings, where they exist, must be eradicated, and wholesome school activities that will provide substitute outlets for the abundant energies of youth should be encouraged. Perhaps as the mores of society change to fit the facts of human nature, the problem will become less acute. There is some indication that this is taking place.

## Homosexuality

Prior to reaching the period of adolescence, both boys and girls (as was pointed out earlier) are primarily interested in members of their own sex. Freud has called this the "latency period," but it might also be called the "homosexual period." During this pre-adolescent period, not only are boys and girls interested in associating with like sex members in most social activities, but overt sexual activities between members of the same sex frequently take place. Kinsey found, for example, that 29 per cent of twelve-year-old boys engage in such homosexual practices as exhibition of genitalia to other boys, mutual manipulation of genitalia, anal or oral contacts with genitalia, and urethral insertions. Among girls, 33 per cent admitted that they had engaged in homosexual play prior to the onset of adolescence. This consisted primarily of genital exhibitions and examinations (99 per cent) and manual manipulation of the genitalia of one or both girls (62 per cent).

With the onset of adolescence, boys and girls become increasingly interested in the other sex. However, there is a carry-over into adolescence and adult life of pre-adolescent homosexual play and activities. By the age of forty-five (according to Kinsey), 37 per cent of American males and 13 per cent of American females have had homosexual experiences leading to orgasm.

These figures are much higher than most people would expect. Homosexuality is thus a serious problem for education and for society in general.

Because of the very nature of homosexuality, society has erected severe taboos against it. Males are particularly singled out for persecution and blackmail, although a somewhat more lenient attitude exists toward female homosexuals. It is common in our culture to see girls and women dancing together or rooming together. Most of these associations are not of a strictly sexual nature, but some of them are. With the population explosion what it is, society probably can get along and increase in numbers regardless of the homosexual element. The individual homosexual, however, is subject to great stress and strain. He is constantly in fear of being detected, and suffers from feelings that he is "abnormal." He doesn't like himself as he is, but doesn't see how he can change himself.

The causes of homosexuality are not entirely clear. Freudians believe that parent-child relationships during the formative years (during the oedipus period) have an important bearing on whether a boy will develop a masculine role and whether a girl will be truly feminine. There is ample evidence, however, from all sources, including the Freudian, that a great share of homosexual behavior is learned. Adolescent boys, for example, who suffer humiliation and lack of success in their associations with girls may turn to boys as the object of their love impulses. Girls who fear pregnancy and are taught that boys are bad may find that a love affair with another girl is much safer than a heterosexual venture.

The school has at least two important functions to perform in assisting the potential homosexual and preventing a wider spread of the practice. The first is to help those pupils with some homosexual feelings or experiences to realize that they are indeed normal individuals. All people, male and female, have hormones of the opposite sex in their blood streams, and all people have characteristics of the other sex in various degrees. Such an assurance will help the individual adolescent to reduce his guilt feelings. Secondly, all boys and girls of adolescent age should be given every opportunity to engage in worthwhile heterosexual activities. Work on the school paper, dramatics, school dances and parties, hikes, and the like will throw young people together in ways that should encourage heterosexual adjustment.

A word of warning should be given to teachers or school counselors who are concerned about the homosexual problem. Students cannot be identified as homosexual by any known physical characteristic. The boy who appears feminine may be extremely masculine, and the boy with a deep voice and heavy beard may be a potential or active homosexual. Only through an interview with the individual who will reveal his feelings and practices, or by direct observation of overt behavior, can the existence of homosexuality be confirmed.

## Sex Education and the Adolescent

Sex education should begin in the home before the child starts to school, should be continued during the elementary school years, and should receive much attention by both the home and the school during the adolescent period. Adolescence brings many new problems of a sexual nature that are of only small concern to the child. In a study made by Oliver Butterfield of the love problems of adolescents, it was found that adolescent boys and girls are greatly concerned with such questions as:

- Is it all right to make a blind date?
- What about pick-up dates?
- Is it all right to park after a school dance?
- Can a brother and sister get a baby?
- What is masturbation?
- Should a student go steady?
- What is true love, and how can one recognize it?
- How much difference should there be in the ages of a boy and girl who are to be married?
- Should a tall girl avoid marrying a tall man, lest she have children who are abnormally tall?
- How far should familiarities increase during engagement?
- Why shouldn't young people feel free to engage in sex relations before marriage if they know safe contraceptive methods?
- Why don't they teach more about sex and social relations in school?

The amount of interest shown by teachers, parents, nonparents, and students in the question of sex education is revealed in a study by Kenneth B. Henderson. Sixty-one Illinois secondary schools and their constituents participated in the investigation. The question asked was: "Should the school help students obtain sound sex education?" All the groups strongly favored instruction in sex education. The percentage of individuals answering "yes" is shown in Table I. As can be seen, over 80 per cent of parents, teachers, and students feel the need for this type of instruction, as do also 77 per cent of the nonparents. In this same study, additional data show that only 10 per cent of the teachers and 20 per cent of the graduates of these secondary schools feel that sufficient attention is being given to sex instruction in the schools. Probably the most effective type of sex-education program would be one that integrates sex-education study into such courses as biology, physiology, health or hygiene, sociology, home economics, civics, and literature, and that also provides a special course dealing with family and personal living problems. Boys need the latter type of course as much as girls, although in many schools it is a course mainly for girls. The course in sex education should be given a nonemotional title such as "personal relations," "life adjustment," or "family living."

TABLE I

*Should the School Help Students Obtain Sound Sex Education?*

*Percentage Answering "Yes"*

| Teachers | Parents | Nonparents | Students |
|---|---|---|---|
| 83 (N = 2024) | 82 (N = 6455) | 77 (N = 1739) | 83 (N = 20101) |

Any program in sex instruction must have the wholehearted support of parents and the rest of the community. The PTA group or other parent group can help in planning the work and can review, from time to time, films and other materials that are to be used in the program. The reader who is interested in more detailed discussion of sex-education programs will find the following references useful:

1. Baker, J. N., *Sex Education in High Schools*. New York: Emerson Books.
2. Baruch, Dorothy W., *New Ways in Sex Education*. New York: McGraw-Hill Book Co.
3. Bibby, Cyril, *Sex Education*. New York: Emerson Books.
4. Crow, Lester D., and Crow, Alice, *Sex Education for the Growing Family*. Boston: Christopher Publishing House.
5. Gruenberg, Benjamin C., *How Can We Teach About Sex?*, Public Affairs Pamphlet, No. 122, Public Affairs Committee, Inc., 22 East 38th Street, New York, New York.

6. Kirkendall, Lester A., and Hamilton, Archie, "Current Practices in Sex Education," *High School Journal*, Vol. 37, pp. 143–148.
7. Strain, Frances B., *Sex Guidance in Family Life Education: A Handbook for the Schools*. New York: The Macmillan Co.

Valuable films that can be used in sex-education programs at the secondary school level have also been produced. Some of the best of these are the McGraw-Hill productions called *Human Reproduction, Physical Aspects of Puberty*, and *Social-Sex Attitudes in Adolescence*. A test with two forms entitled *Sex Knowledge Inventories*, published by Family Life Publications, Durham, North Carolina, is also available for use. Materials that have been especially prepared for use by the boys and girls themselves include *Facts of Life and Love*, by Evelyn Duvall, and *Youth Grown into Adulthood*, by Morey Fields and others.

## Readings for Further Study

Butterfield, O. M., *Love Problems of Adolescents*. New York: Emerson Books, 1941.

Henderson, K. B., *Principal Findings of the Follow-Up Study of the Illinois Secondary School Curriculum Program*, Superintendent of Public Instruction, Springfield, Illinois, 1952.

Himelhoch, Jerome, and Fava, Sylvia F., eds., *Sexual Behavior in American Society*. New York: W. W. Norton & Co., 1955.

Kinsey, Alfred C., *et al.*, *Sexual Behavior in the Human Male*. Philadelphia: W. B. Saunders Co., 1948.

Kinsey, Alfred C., *et al.*, *Sexual Behavior in the Human Female*. Philadelphia: W. B. Saunders Co., 1953.

Ramsey, Glenn V., "The Sex Information of Younger Boys," in J. M. Seidman, ed., *The Adolescent—A Book of Readings*, rev. ed. New York: Holt, Rinehart & Winston, 1960, pp. 333–339.

Schneiders, Alexander A., *Personality Development and Adjustment in Adolescence*. Milwaukee: Bruce Publishing Co., 1961, Chapter 6.

"Student Sex Standards and Behavior: The Educator's Responsibility," *Journal of the National Association of Women Deans and Counselors*, Vol. 26, No. 2, January, 1963, pp. 1–52. (This entire issue is devoted to sex problems of late adolescence.)

Whyte, W. F., "A Slum Sex Code," in J. M. Seidman, ed., *The Adolescent—A Book of Readings*, rev. ed., New York: Holt, Rinehart & Winston, 1960, pp. 348–359.

# 10

# Personal Problems of the Adolescent

IT IS INEVITABLE that young people will have many problems and worries as they make the difficult transition from childhood to adulthood. Mastering the developmental tasks referred to in Chapter 1 is not easy; hence, adolescents need much help if they are to develop into stable and useful adult citizens. Chief among those who are in a strategic position to help adolescents solve their problems and alleviate their worries are secondary school teachers and guidance counselors. In this chapter some of the problems that perpetually vex adolescents and perplex the adults who deal with them will be listed, and suggestions for helping the adolescent to solve them will be given.

## PROBLEMS OF EARLY- AND LATE-MATURING ADOLESCENTS

Professor Harold E. Jones and associates at the University of California have made an extensive study of the special problems that face early- and late-maturing adolescents. They found that early-maturing girls suffer real handicaps, and that early-maturing boys are not adversely affected but, in fact, are benefited by early physical and sexual development. As for girls, early development results in their feeling conspicuous at a time when conspicuousness is not valued. Many find themselves embarrassingly tall and heavy and possessed of greater breast development than they consider normal for their ages. The early-maturing girl naturally is interested in boys, but the boys of her age or school grade, on the average, are three or four years behind her in physical development and are hence unreceptive.

If the early-maturing girl tries to find associates among the older boys of her school or neighborhood, she encounters other difficulties. Most parents do not want their eleven- or twelve-year-old daughter dating boys who are fifteen or sixteen. Thus, she is caught in a dilemma. If she remains with her own age group, she is frustrated; if she moves into a group much older than she, her lack of judgment and social maturity can create serious social problems, as well as the guilt feelings she may experience if she disobeys her parents' wishes.

To some extent these problems are accentuated by the age-grade systems generally used in our public schools. The early-maturing girl would not be nearly so conspicuous in an ungraded type of program or, in fact, in the old-fashioned country school where children of all ages were in one room. Some authorities have suggested that girls be allowed to enter the first grade of our schools a year earlier than boys. This, of course, would reduce the developmental disparity between the sexes by one year during the remaining years of the school program.

While early-maturing girls have many serious adjustment problems to face, this is not generally so with late-maturing girls. The studies show that late-maturing girls are superior in many respects to both early-maturing girls and girls who mature at an average age. In the Harold Jones study, the late maturers, on the average, were superior to other girls in personal appearance, poise, cheerfulness, sociability, leadership, and prestige. This advantage is probably partly due to the fact that a longer growing period allows for a more balanced physical development. Late-maturing girls also have longer legs than other girls, which adds to their beauty, according to American standards. Furthermore, the late-maturing girl is more nearly in step with the development of boys in her age group. Thus, her interests in mixed social activities can be more readily satisfied.

When we consider the problems of the late-maturing boy, we find a complete reversal of the situation that exists for late-maturing girls. The slow-maturing boy is too small to gain acceptance in athletics; he is too immature to get dates with girls his own age. He frequently develops inferiority feelings that may persist for a lifetime.

School teachers and counselors should do everything in their power to reassure late-maturing boys that when they reach maturity they will be as tall as earlier-maturing boys and that their rates of growth are perfectly normal. It is important that late-maturing boys not try to adjust by withdrawing from competition and becoming submissive and self-effacing. If late-maturing boys can gain a sufficient feeling of security, many of them will also be less noisy and aggressive and less prone to seek excessive attention.

## PROBLEMS RESULTING FROM PHYSICAL DEVIATIONS FROM THE NORM

It has already been mentioned that early-maturing girls and late-maturing boys suffer from anxieties and worries partly because their physiques vary from the norms of their age mates. Many studies show that practically all adolescents, regardless of their rate of development, are very sensitive about physical defects and somatic variations. Boys and girls worry because they feel they are too thin or too heavy, too tall or too short, or that their hips are too wide or their legs too big. Of great concern to adolescents is their facial appearance. Some of the facial characteristics that worry adolescents are blackheads and pimples, lack of beard, heavy eyebrows, scars, birthmarks, moles, irregular teeth, heavy lips, protruding chin, protruding ears, oily skin, freckles, having to wear glasses, dark skin, and a too long or odd-shaped nose.

Many adolescents would change themselves physically if they could. In a study made in Arizona by Frazier and Lisonbee, two-thirds of all adolescents queried wished to change their appearance in one way or another. Following are some of the verbatim statements of the boys.

I would make my chest bigger than it is now and also my shoulders. I would like to weigh a little bit more, say about twenty to twenty-five pounds more.

I would make myself look handsomer and not fat. I would have wavy black hair. I would change my whole physical appearance so that I would be handsome with a good build.

Well, I would start off by putting on some meat, next I would get rid of my pimples, then get some muscles, then get rid of my glasses.

The way adolescent girls feel about physical deviations can be seen by some of their comments:

My hips and legs are too large and fat. If I could have smaller hips and legs, I'd have a much better figure. I'd also like to be a little more developed above the waist than I am, but I am not too flat. I wish I didn't have so many pimples or have to wear glasses.

I would first of all change my nose, as it is large. I think some day I will go to a plastic surgeon and get my nose changed. . . . I would like a clear, unscarred complexion. I have blackheads and pimples. I may go to a dermatologist.

I would like to be three inches shorter and have smaller feet.

There is no question that many adolescents consider themselves to be abnormal in physical characteristics when in reality they are well within the normal range. For example, girls are sometimes known to worry because their menstrual cycles vary from the so-called norm of 28 days. A study made by Fluhmann[1] of 76 healthy young women showed that their menstrual cycles varied from 11 to 144 days, the great majority falling between 18 and 42 days. Only five of the girls showed absolutely regular cycles. A certain amount of variation is to be expected. Marked deviations, of course, should be checked, and a metabolism test should be made by a qualified physician, who may recommend medication.

Adolescent boys are known to be sometimes concerned about the size of their genital organs and to develop personality disorders because of their anxieties. Yet, such concern in most cases is groundless, because the boys are in all likelihood well within the limits of normality. If adolescent boys and girls could be supplied with appropriate information regarding the great range of individual differences that typically exists among individuals of their age, a great deal of personal unhappiness could be eliminated. The teacher, psychological counselor, or athletic coach is

[1] This research reported in the 43rd yearbook of the National Society for the Study of Education, Part I, University of Chicago, 1944, pp. 29–30.

in a position to offer sympathetic help and advice to adolescents who are distressed because of real or imagined physical defects or somatic deviations.

## OTHER WORRIES AND PROBLEMS

The basic insecurity of adolescents stemming partly from the ambiguous status they hold in our society leads to problems and worries in many additional areas. Adolescents are concerned and anxious regarding problems of courtship, sex, marriage, religion, family relationships, school progress, educational and vocational futures, and personality development.

A very thorough investigation of the problems that trouble adolescents was carried out in Illinois by Harold C. Hand and associates.[2] Seven thousand twelfth-grade pupils in 57 high schools were administered the Mooney *Problem Check List.* This questionnaire contains 330 problems that often bother adolescents. In the Illinois study the students were instructed to answer the questions anonymously, so that an honest opinion of their chief worries and problems would be revealed. Some of the problems checked by 25 per cent or more of the boys were "military service," "how to dance," "how to save money," "what I'll be ten years hence," "dull classes," "too little study time," "weak spelling and grammar," and "occupational decision."

Over 25 per cent of the girls checked such items as "afraid of making mistakes," "daydreaming," "losing my temper," "worry about grades," "want better personality," "afraid to speak in class," "have less money than friends do," "too easily hurt," and "overweight."

At the end of the Mooney *Problem Check List,* space is provided for each student to summarize his chief problems in his own words. A few of the verbatim statements made by twelfth-grade boys and girls follow:

I would very much like to become a teacher, but since I am not working and it costs money to go to college, the future doesn't look so good. I also worry about whether I will find the right mate. [a girl]

---

[2] Harold C. Hand, *Principal Findings of the 1947–48 Basic Studies of the Illinois Secondary School Curriculum Program,* Superintendent of Public Instruction, Springfield, Illinois, 1949, pp. 67–73.

I am especially worried because not only are my religious beliefs confused but my life is quite opposite to that which I feel a Christian should lead. Moreover, although I would like to change certain things in my life, I don't seem to have the will power to do so, especially as all my friends' lives are very similar to mine. [a girl]

My chief problem deals with my disappointment in one love affair. I worry about this because many of the fellows think an ex-engaged girl isn't all she could be. They take advantage of you and expect too much.

I am always troubled about my subjects and worried that my grades are not high enough. I think the teachers are too strict with their grades and we don't have enough freedom in class. [a boy]

My home life is the source of most of my troubles. My parents do not get along very well. [a girl]

My chief trouble is woman trouble. I go steady with one, but like another better. I am not sure what I should do or how I should do it. [a boy]

I am altogether too shy. I want to date the girls but I am too shy or scared. One reason is I don't have enough money available.

I am too concerned about being in love and holding that person. Also I am confused on my moral code as everyone seems to have a different idea of what is wrong and what is right. [a girl]

My chief problem is sex and learning to control my urges. [a girl]

I have a feeling that I am always being watched and am always in the wrong even though I didn't do anything. [a girl]

I have got a low IQ. I am full of faults. I should have checked more problems and worries than I did. [a boy]

## The Problem of Being Normal

When the thousands of worries that beset adolescents are analyzed, one outstanding trend emerges. It is that adolescents want to be normal human beings. To be different is usually considered a bad thing. This is probably a general human trait, but the urge to conform or to be normal seems to be accentuated during adolescence.

Since one definition of "normal" is to be at the "norm," or "average," and since in statistics the "average" is a mathematical number or point, it is obvious that few, if any, adolescents can be really normal, according to this definition. Half will be above average, and the other half will be below. This will apply to any trait that might be mentioned. Weights of adolescents will be too high or too low; breasts will be too large or too small; noses will be too long or too short; feet will be too big or too little; IQs will be too high or too low, and so on.

In dealing with adolescents, it is most important that a different concept of normality from the one defined above be used. No adolescent wants to be thought of as being abnormal. Teachers, counselors, and others who work with children and young people, or other people for that matter, might well take the position that *anyone who falls under the normal curve is normal.*[3] This, of course, includes everyone, for 100 per cent of a distribution will be found under the bell-shaped normal curve. To be different, then, is to be normal. It takes all kinds of people to satisfy this criterion of normality. It is perfectly normal for a high school senior boy to be four feet, eight inches tall, although he is obviously short. It is likewise normal for a girl to be six feet tall. Many are that tall, and if it were not for these tall girls, we would not have a normal curve. Similarly, it is exceedingly normal for an adolescent to have an IQ of 75. Hundreds of thousands of pupils have IQs in this neighborhood, and this value, of course, falls under the normal curve.

No harm can possibly result from persuading each adolescent to feel that he is normal. This will reduce many worries and lessen tensions. After he is reassured that he is normal, then various diagnostic tests or other measures can be used to appraise his achievements, interests, or talents. A profile of his traits can be obtained that will show just what his "normality" looks like. If he is weak in some area, he can be encouraged to improve that particular aspect of his knowledge or personality. If his complete profile shows that he deviates considerably from the average in some physical attribute that is not subject to change or learning, he can at least view his status as being very normal.

This author has interviewed many adolescents who were depressed, discouraged, and worried because they thought they were abnormal in some way. When they were shown that their characteristics fell under the normal curve of distribution, a great load was lifted. Some of them remarked, "This is the first time

---

[3] This definition would obviously not apply to diseases and some severe physical defects.

that I ever knew I was normal." With the pressure and anxiety gone, the student is then in good mental shape to be given sound teaching or educational and vocational guidance that is in line with his achievements, interests, and other traits.

Some who read the foregoing approach to counseling worried adolescents may view this interpretation of normality as being only a psychological trick that can produce effective results and lessen anxieties. There is no question that this approach will reduce worries and anxieties, but it is not entirely a trick. It is a novel interpretation of what normality means, which at the same time takes away the stigma of being "abnormal" when one is really only different.

The preceding discussion of what it means to be normal has definite implications for junior and senior high schools that group their adolescents for instructional purposes. Many schools desire to have at least three levels of instruction in subjects such as reading, mathematics, or science for pupils of a given age or grade level. They want one class for pupils who are low in achievement in the subject, another class or classes for so-called regular achievers, and a third type of class for pupils who are accelerated in the subject. This is a very good idea and is in line with what is known about readiness for learning. Pupils who are homogeneously grouped on the basis of achievement or interest can be better taught than in a group that is too heterogeneous. However, if being placed in a special class implies that a pupil is abnormal or dull, more harm than good usually results.

There is no reason, however, that every pupil in every class in the junior or senior high school, regardless of the level of instruction in the class, cannot be made to feel that he is normal. He can be told that he is very normal and at the same time be informed that he needs special instruction, say, in reading. He will undoubtedly agree with this. He knows that he does not read well, and in most cases he will desire to improve his skills if no stigma is attached to the process. The teacher of a special reading class can point out that anyone can learn to read, just as anyone can learn to tap-dance or play the piccolo. The teacher may cite the cases of famous men, such as President Andrew Johnson who learned to read after he was married.

The school that desires to make all students feel normal and confident should seldom use so-called intelligence tests as a basis of grouping. In fact, secondary schools would probably be much better off if so-called intelligence tests were not given in the schools at all. These tests do not measure potential ability to do schoolwork well, and in addition they serve in a tremendous number of cases to humiliate and stigmatize pupils and parents. This does not mean that schools should abandon a thorough testing program. Achievement and interest tests serve an extremely valuable function in teaching. The best single indicator of future achievement in an area of instruction is present achievement. "Intelligence tests" themselves are nothing but achievement tests, but they are so general in scope that they make an extremely poor basis for grouping pupils for a specific learning task. The fact that they also imply that they measure native mental ability makes them particularly pernicious when used by schools. Achievement, interest, and aptitude tests for various areas do not have this unfortunate connotation.

## Readings for Further Study

Frazier, Alexander, and Lisonbee, Lorenzo K., "Adolescent Concerns with Physique," *The School Review*, Vol. 58, pp. 397–405.

Harris, Dale B., "Sex Differences in the Life Problems of Adolescents, 1935 and 1957," Chapter 11 in Victor H. Noll and Rachel P. Noll, eds., *Readings in Educational Psychology*. New York: The Macmillan Co., 1962.

Jones, Harold E., "Adolescence in Our Society," in J. M. Seidman, ed., *The Adolescent: A Book of Readings*, rev. ed. New York: Holt, Rinehart & Winston, 1960, pp. 50–60.

Lorand, Sandor, and Schneer, Henry I., *Adolescents: Psychoanalytical Approach to Problems and Therapy*. New York: Paul B. Hoeber, Inc., 1961, Chapters 3, 4, 5, 9, 10.

Mohr, George J., and Despres, Marian A., *The Stormy Decade: Adolescence*. New York: Random House, 1958, Chapters 12, 13, 14.

Remmers, H. H., and Radler, D. H., *The American Teenager*. Indianapolis–New York: Bobbs-Merrill Co., 1957, Chapters 3, 6.

Strang, Ruth, *The Adolescent Views Himself*. New York: McGraw-Hill Book Co., 1957, Chapter 4.

# 11

# Adolescent Disciplinary Problems

MANY JUNIOR and senior high school teachers consider the keeping of discipline in the classroom to be their number-one professional problem. Some teachers claim that it is impossible for them to discipline many of the larger boys. These teachers constantly send the most troublesome cases to the principal's office. Other teachers feel that they can control any classroom situation by use of threats, assignment of extra work, and physical force, provided they show the pupils who is boss at the first class meeting. They admit that it is a difficult task, but as long as they do not turn their backs to the class, everything goes reasonably well.

Other methods that teachers have used to maintain discipline include use of sarcasm, changing the seating arrangement, failing pupils in the course, and putting pupils in "solitary confinement" (that is, removing them to a part of the room where there are no other pupils).

Most of these methods are obviously police methods, or methods that are used in some penal institutions. Of course, if a teacher feels that his work is primarily that of a policeman rather than a promoter of learning, he may not see anything particularly out of line with such approaches to discipline.

Many teachers today, however, are reasonably well trained

in psychology and understand the basic processes of adjustment described in Chapter 2 of this book. They realize that pupils are not naturally bad or depraved, but are individuals who have needs that must be met in one way or another. Whenever a pupil misbehaves, the teacher should ask himself certain questions. What is the pupil gaining by this particular behavior? Which fundamental need is being satisfied by doing what he is doing? Teachers should realize that there are causes behind every type of behavior exhibited by pupils.

In a surprising number of schools, a typical method of dealing with misdeeds is to keep the offending pupils after school for a variable number of minutes depending upon the nature of the "crime." If a pupil is tardy, he is kept after school; if he doesn't do his history assignment, he is kept after school; if he whispers, he is kept after school; if he throws paper wads, he is kept after school. There is clearly no connection in these instances between the offenses and the punishment. This procedure is similar to that followed by doctors of an earlier period who prescribed little pink pills for their patients regardless of what ailed them.

If a pupil is tardy, the teacher should try to find out why. Perhaps the family does not own an alarm clock. Maybe the pupil works before school, or the mother is ill and he must do the dishes. If the pupil doesn't do his history lesson, the teacher again should try to find out the reason. Perhaps he cannot read, or has lost his book. Maybe he doesn't see how studying history will do him any good anyway. If he whispers, there is a reason, also. Perhaps he has nothing to do. Maybe the work is too difficult for him. Perhaps he is uninterested or bored. It could be that he whispers to attract attention. Or he might be whispering to find the answer to an important question that will help him with his work. If a pupil throws paper wads, there are also specific motivations involved. People just do not throw paper wads for nothing. Some pupils secure in this manner attention and recognition that is denied them in more legitimate activities. If a pupil cannot succeed in conjugating French verbs, he may achieve distinction among his peers as being the roughest and toughest pupil in the room. Other pupils will look up to him. That makes him somebody.

## Some Other Types of Misbehavior

### THE PUPIL WHO STEALS

*212 73*

Behind the act of stealing there are always causes or motives. The teacher should try to find out what needs the pupil is satisfying with this type of behavior. A pupil may steal because he is hungry or needs clothes, or because he needs money to impress his friends. Perhaps he can purchase the social approval of his peers if he has money to buy gifts for them. Sometimes pupils steal in order to get revenge upon another pupil or the teacher, or to vent hostile feelings toward their parents. Just what should be done in the case of a pupil who steals would depend upon which of the foregoing motives were operative. The pupil who steals because he is hungry should certainly, first of all, be supplied the necessities of life. The pupil who steals in order to buy gifts that will win him acceptance into a social group needs help in gaining social recognition in other ways. The pupil who steals because of hostility toward his teacher probably needs more affection and response from the teacher and an opportunity to release his emotions in such activities as school plays, music, art, or athletics. From the mental-hygiene point of view, it is very unwise to demand a confession from the pupil who steals, or to publicly accuse him of such an act. Such procedures do not get at the basic cause of his trouble, and may only aggravate the case by causing him to lie or gain a bad reputation for an act he may not commit again.

### THE PUPIL WHO CHEATS

Cheating on school examinations and in other written work is a problem that confronts a great many teachers. It is true, however, that pupils cheat in the classes of some teachers and not in others. Pupils cheat for a variety of reasons. Some possible causes for this behavior are: (1) the task may be too difficult, (2) too high a premium may be placed upon marks or grades rather than on understanding, and (3) the pupil may feel inadequate or insecure in the classroom situation.

The pupil who cheats is usually under severe pressure to make good, or has a fear that he will fail in his studies. The teacher who gears learning tasks to the abilities and interests of pupils will find that cheating drops off drastically. Many times pupils do not see how the subject they are studying will help them personally. They therefore take the shortest possible route to secure a passing grade. Schoolwork directly related to real-life activities often so intrigues pupils that the possibility of cheating never occurs to them. Much cheating can, however, be expected in dull and tense classes in which a premium is placed upon the acquisition of material that has doubtful value in the minds of the pupils. Even in such situations the honor system, as employed by some schools, has had a marked effect in reducing cheating. When pupils are given responsibility for their own conduct and when peer group pressures are brought to bear, it is a rare pupil who will break the rules of the game. Under the honor system there may be thirty or forty pairs of watchful eyes supervising an examination instead of just the teacher's one pair of eyes.

## THE TRUANT

The truant is a pupil who just does not want to go to school and makes plans to do something else. He may go fishing, attend a movie, visit the circus, take a trip, or work on some interesting project in a friend's basement. If the activities at school challenged him as much as those outside school, it is certain that he would be no truant. Basketball coaches seldom have problems of truancy among their players. In fact, they often have great difficulty keeping the boys out of the gymnasium even when practices are not scheduled. The pupil who is successful in school— whose needs are being met—is unhappy if events prevent him from attending his classes. Teachers should consider truancy as a sign that something is wrong with the school. When changes have been made in school programs, truancy has been known to drop off. One teacher commented upon one of his pupils as follows: "K is one of our truants. We have previously had great difficulty in keeping him in school. He is now in one of the remedial-reading clubs, where he is responsible for telling the other pupils when the group meets. His truancy first disappeared on the days the club met, but recently he has been attending school every day." This boy cannot afford to be absent from school, because he would then miss the opportunity of being a valued member of his reading club.

## How Teachers Handle Some Disciplinary Problems

### A CLASSROOM SHOW-OFF

Mr. Gordon was teaching his first day in a medium-sized high school. The subject was Algebra I. Mr. Gordon began to call the roll. All went well until he came to the name of Harry Shields. When he called this name, a large unkempt-looking boy waved his arms in the air and shouted with ear-splitting volume, "I'm here, see? I'm right here. Old Harry Shields is right here." The rest of the students began to laugh, and general disorder temporarily swept over the classroom. The next day when the roll was called, the same incident took place. Mr. Gordon then sent the pupils to the blackboard to do some problems. Harry again began to talk in loud tones that could be heard all over the classroom and even in adjoining rooms. Mr. Gordon was greatly worried about what to do. He did not show it, however. Instead, he spoke to Harry privately, and asked him if he could come in for a chat during a conference hour the next morning. Harry was told that all the pupils in the class would be asked to make similar visits. Harry said he would come, and, sure enough, he kept his appointment.

When Harry entered Mr. Gordon's office for his private conference, the first thing he said was, "You know, I'm a pretty tough customer. I ran a teacher out of the high school I attended last year." Mr. Gordon made no comment. Harry went on talking. He said, "You know, I have a very loud voice." Mr. Gordon replied that he didn't particularly mind loud noises, as he used to work in a machine shop and had become accustomed to noise. Harry then said, "You know, I can also speak softly if I want to." Mr. Gordon did not comment directly, but gave the impression that he was not particularly concerned with how loudly a pupil spoke. He told Harry that he just wanted to get acquainted and help him plan his future or assist him with any problem he might have. He also told Harry that he thought it was unnecessary to call the roll every day, and wondered if it wouldn't be better to make a seating chart as a means of checking on class attendance. Harry agreed that this might be a good idea. Mr. Gordon then asked Harry if he would be willing to take charge of the seating chart for the ensuing week. Harry consented to do this.

The next day, Harry took over his duties in connection with the class roll. His behavior changed remarkably. Mr. Gordon reported to this author that, from that time on, Harry ceased entirely his loud talking and became a very cooperative pupil.

## STUDY-HALL DISORDER

Madison High School had a very serious study-hall problem. Miss Henderson, the teacher in charge, was doing her best to provide a quiet place for pupils to study, but her efforts were futile. On one occasion a mouse was brought into the room and released. On another, a "stink bomb" was burst. During such periods the entire study hall was in an uproar. Miss Henderson's procedure was to try to locate the culprit in each case. She would dash to the section of the room where the disorder seemed to break out, and would look for a pupil who gave the appearance of being guilty. When she spotted a promising suspect, she would pounce upon him and give him a good shaking or send him from the room. The pupils loved this, for seldom did she ever apprehend the real culprit. When she could not find a guilty-looking pupil, she would turn upon the whole group with threatening statements of what she would do if such disorder should break out again.

Each study-hall period began to degenerate into an exciting game of seeing what Miss Henderson would do next. She tried to police the room, but it was so large and there were so many pupils that she simply could not cover her "beat." Finally, one day Miss Henderson did not appear at school. The principal received a report that she had had a nervous breakdown and probably would be gone for the rest of the year.

A new teacher was brought in to take over the study hall—a Miss Raymond. Miss Raymond's concepts of disciplinary methods differed radically from those of Miss Henderson. After introducing herself to the pupils, Miss Raymond explained that she had no fixed ideas on just how a study hall should be run. She said that she wanted the type of conditions and atmosphere in the study hall that were desired by the pupils. She asked them if they would like to elect a committee to draw up procedures that all could follow. The pupils liked the idea, and suggested that the elected committee submit its tentative plan, when finished, to all the pupils in the study hall for their approval or amendment. This course of action was carried out, and rules of conduct for the study hall were developed entirely by the pupils. Miss Raymond then made it clear that she was not at all interested in serving as an officer to carry out the rules that the pupils had enacted. She suggested that the pupils design a system for enforcing the rules they had made. The pupils set about to do this, and finally came forward with a system that included a standing committee on study-hall procedure. A separate committee was elected for each period of the day. Pupils who were dissatisfied with any condition existing in the study hall were encouraged to report their grievances to this committee, which would then recommend appropriate action. Membership on this committee was rotated in such a way that many pupils were given the opportunity to serve. Cases of improper study hall conduct were vigorously dealt with by this committee. Strong social pressure soon developed among the pupils to maintain a place of study that was in line with their expressed wishes.

Many suggestions for improving the physical appearance and educational facilities of the study hall were also sent in to the committee from time to time by pupils. As a result, bookshelves were built along one entire wall of the previously bare hall, and these were filled with newspapers, magazines, and numerous interesting books. Some movable tables and chairs were added, and potted plants were placed in appropriate places. The pupils began to take an interest in their study hall. So far as discipline was concerned, it ceased to be any real problem at all. Miss Raymond continued to work in the study hall, but her duties consisted of helping pupils with whatever problems they cared to bring to her. She worked *with* the pupils, not against them.

## DESTRUCTION OF SCHOOL PROPERTY

When pupils and teachers arrived at Union High School one morning, they found the building and the white pillars at the entrance smeared with red paint. Several light globes in front of the school were also broken. Investigation produced evidence that this was the work of Jim Duncan, a high school sophomore who was considered a general nuisance around school. When confronted with the evidence, Jim admitted his guilt but was unable to give a reason for his behavior. A group of teachers met with the principal that evening after school to decide what to do with Jim. It was suggested by several teachers that Jim was "no good," and that there was no use putting up with him any longer. A recommendation was made that he be expelled from school. One teacher, however, vigorously disagreed with the group, and refused to concur in this recommendation. She stated that in her opinion Jim was a boy who had been beaten down around school, had been unsuccessful in his studies, and had received nothing in the way of commendation for even a few small efforts he had made to do well. She maintained that his desire for recognition and status had been almost entirely thwarted in every avenue of the school's activities. "What Jim needs," she said, "is a chance to be significant in some activity connected with the school." What activity this might be she was unable to say. One of the other teachers, however, now came to the rescue and stated that there was a need for an assistant to help the regular custodian of the building. Some small compensation would be made available for this work. After much discussion, it was agreed that this idea be presented to Jim for his reaction. This was done, and Jim accepted the job with great enthusiasm. The principal who related this incident to this author stated that the morning after Jim had received the appointment, he arrived at the school building one hour before classes began and insisted that every pupil wipe off his shoes before entering the building. Jim had now found an activity that satisfied his need for attention and status. He ceased to present a disciplinary problem.

## Principles for Keeping Discipline

Teachers should realize that adolescents (and anyone else, for that matter) generally behave in about the only way possible for them to behave, considering the hereditary characteristics they possess, the experiences they have had, and the needs and social pressures operating upon them at the moment. This is another way of saying that *behavior is caused.* This statement also indicates some of the causes. This principle implies that teachers have an opportunity to alter the behavior of adolescents by helping them restructure their environment and by creating new social arrangements. Many a problem pupil has developed into a good school citizen after being introduced and admitted to a social group with high ideals.

Disciplinary problems inevitably arise when schools do not fit their curriculums to the needs and abilities of all the pupils enrolled.

Eight generalizations and suggestions for maintaining good classroom morale and effective discipline follow:

1. Praise and social approval are more important in promoting good standards of conduct than are censure, blame, and punishment.
2. It is unwise to penalize a whole group for the misbehavior of an individual or a small group.
3. Sarcasm is not an effective tool. Pupils are sensitive, and may be severely hurt by this procedure.
4. The teacher should never consider misconduct as a personal affront. Instead, he should adopt the attitude that his interests and those of the student go in the same direction.
5. Whenever possible, rules and regulations should be formulated by the pupils, or by the pupils working with the teacher.

6. Discipline is very difficult to maintain unless pupils sense that the activities in which they engage have real worth for them.

7. Whenever disciplinary problems arise, the teacher should ask himself: What is wrong with the course of study? What is wrong with my teaching methods?

8. Some pupils who misbehave may be physically ill or be suffering from a glandular disorder. The aid of the school nurse or physician should be enlisted in dealing with such cases.

# Readings for Further Study

Amsterdam, Ruth, *Constructive Classroom Discipline and Practice*. New York: Comet Press Books, 1957.

Canning, Ray R., "Does an Honor System Reduce Classroom Cheating? An Experimental Answer," *Journal of Experimental Education*, Vol. 24, pp. 291–296.

Kounin, Jacob S., Gump, Paul V., and Ryan, James J., "Explorations in Classroom Management," *Journal of Teacher Education*, Vol. 12, pp. 235–246.

Sheviakov, George V., and Redl, Fritz, *Discipline for Today's Children and Youth*. Washington, D. C.: Association for Supervision and Curriculum Development, N.E.A., 1956.

Wittenberg, Rudolph M., *Adolescence and Discipline*. New York: Association Press, 1959, Chapter 14.

Woodruff, Asahel D., "Discipline," in *Encyclopedia of Educational Research*, 3rd ed., 1960, pp. 381–385.

# 12

# Adolescent Delinquency

NEARLY EVERYONE who works with young people has a theory about the growing incidence of criminality among the teenage population. These theories often do little more than expand a given individual's own dissatisfactions and confusions about the complex society in which we live. Sometimes they are nostalgic views of the past. "When I was a boy, no one ever 'talked back' to his parents," or "I had to walk three miles to school every day, and when I came home at night, I had to milk three cows." A similar theme is contained in the oft-stated views that "we are too soft with our children; what they need is stern discipline, and when they 'go bad' they should be punished, not given probation." Other voices are raised against "momism" (too much of mother's protection), schoolwork that is not challenging, schoolwork that is too difficult, availability of too much spending money, the free use of the automobile, the dissolution of the family, the status-seeking life of suburbia, trends toward greater conformity in our society, too much or too little freedom, lurid themes of sex and violence in the mass media, and lack of "old-time religion."

More than anything else, these disparate opinions should convince us that delinquency is not a unitary kind of behavior. Instead, it is a blanket term used to describe a multitude of behaviors with a variety of motivational elements and individual meanings. Most authorities in the field agree that the legal definition of delinquency embraces such a variety of kinds of behavior that no single approach to the problem is likely to be very successful.

## Varieties of Delinquency

Clearly, to the delinquent the personal meaning of aggressive acts such as vandalism or assault is different from that of falsifying one's age in order to buy beer, or engaging in illicit sex activity. Moreover, one individual's act of stealing may have behind it quite a different motive than another's. A single act such as arson may have a variety of meanings. To one young person it may be the result of a neurotic condition linked with the sex drive. To another it might be a wild burst of revenge—getting even with someone who hurt him. To still another it could be the means of asserting himself—of showing that he has power. Or it could be a simple prank that got out of hand. In trying to arrive at a scheme for classifying delinquency types, one might refer to kinds of crimes committed, or to the various types of adolescents who commit crimes, or to the various motive-personality conditions that lead to criminal activity.

It seems logical to this author to classify delinquency according to the meaning of the behavior to the individual and society. The following categories seem to emerge.

### NORM BEHAVIOR

Many kinds of behavior judged by law as illegal are no more than a reflection of behavior judged to be normal by the subculture or the gang to which an adolescent belongs. "Swiping" things, minor vandalism, street fighting, breaking of traffic laws, and purchase of cigarettes and liquor are all normal behavior for certain groups of young people. Such crimes do not represent any deep-seated emotional problems. More often than not, they reflect flaws in our culture—failures to provide the stable kind of community and family life necessary for making the culture's modal values acceptable to all groups.

### EMOTIONAL BEHAVIOR

Within all cultural groups there are individuals whose emotional disturbance manifests itself in some form of aggression or hostility. Youthful crimes of violence such as assault, vandalism, or armed robbery are behaviors the roots of which lie in the life history of a child who has been thwarted and whose conflicts are being resolved through negativistic behavior. Delinquents of this type come from all social classes and cultural groups. The only difference is that for upper-middle-class and upper-class adolescents, such crimes may not be recorded, and hence may be thought of as hidden delinquency. In one study of 6,416 infractions, of which 616 were serious crimes, only 95 became matters of official complaint, and in only 68 was some action taken by the courts.

## PATHOLOGICAL BEHAVIOR

Very serious emotional and mental disturbance may eventuate in behavior of a criminal nature (obviously not all mental illness leads to criminal activity). As previously noted, arson may reflect a neurotic condition in which the compulsion for setting fires is linked to perverted sexual impulses. People with psychopathic or sociopathic personalities may commit shocking crimes, such as multiple murders, seemingly with little compunction or regret.

Among other pathological types should be included mentally defective adolescents, especially those who are culturally deprived. The St. Louis *Post Dispatch* of December 9, 1962, carried a story of two seventeen-year-old boys who robbed and raped a woman and then assaulted her by striking her several times in the head with a baseball bat. They left her in an empty lot, where she was discovered still alive. She was then taken to a hospital, where she lingered unconscious for about two weeks and finally died. Both these adolescents were from large families. The fathers had left the families, and the mothers struggled alone to raise six and eleven children, respectively. One of the boys was mentally retarded. Both had previous records of trouble with the police, one case going back to early childhood.

Of the three types of delinquency just discussed, by far the greatest number of incidents should be subsumed under the category of emotional behavior. Most delinquency is neither the normal "prank" nor the extreme pathological condition.

## Predisposing Psychological and Social Factors

Delinquency is learned behavior. No longer is there much support for the belief that antisocial behavior springs from such innate factors as "moral feeble-mindedness" or instinctual criminal tendencies. Nor is there much foundation for the belief that delinquents are seriously mentally ill (a few of them are, of course, as noted in the previous section). On the other hand, there is overwhelming evidence that delinquency is often accompanied by emotional disturbance, and many believe that criminality is but one of many symptoms of this emotional disturbance. That is, delinquency is a symptom, just as excessive daydreaming, enuresis, and nail-biting are symptoms.

Most delinquents are deprived or frustrated young people who react to the inconsistencies or thwarting of the adult world with aggression. The delinquent who is deprived of affection and a stable and secure world, and who is accorded no status by his group or achieves no feeling of importance, may well be a child who has tried to attain these prized goals in many ways before he finally resorted to aggressive or antisocial behavior.

Much of the activity we call delinquency provides the young person with a feeling of significance. He is simply doing things that are accepted by his group as marks of distinction. All of us crave social significance. If we can find the barriers that prevent us from achieving it, we shall go a long way toward reducing the need for delinquency.

We must credit to the adult world much of the distorted notions of what constitutes significant behavior. Excessive materialism, blatant reports of sex indiscretions, and the association of masculine virility with drinking alcohol are but a few examples of the false values and distorted notions of significance that our adult society builds for young people.

Both teachers and parents must be aware that limited opportunities allow too many of our youth no feeling of accomplishment or personal worth. The boy who finds little success in school is often placed in an overwhelming dilemma. School denies him success, employment opportunities are practically nonexistent for his age group, and there is little he can do around home. Only one avenue remains open—loafing, gang activity, and very possibly crime.

Some of the psychological mechanisms that appear to be involved in delinquency follow.

## IDENTIFICATION

All of us identify with various groups and causes. The adolescent, especially, is prone to ally himself with others of his own age and inclination. In this process, not only does he play a special role in the group or gang, but he also, more than likely, identifies with the causes and with the roles that are created for him by the larger society of young people. He is, in a sense, told how he should be by the images that are given him in newspapers, movies, television, and by word of mouth from others in the group.

## NEGATIVE EMOTIONAL OVERGENERALIZATION

Once there is negative emotional conditioning to a specific person or symbol, similar persons or symbols elicit the same response. The child who hates one policeman may hate all policemen, and indeed all other symbols of authority. Some communities have found that when police serve as referees or coaches in athletic contests, the overgeneralized hostile reaction is dissipated. Similarly, teachers in underprivileged neighborhoods have discovered a decided improvement in behavior when they are able to alter the perception of themselves as authority figures.

## LOWERED THRESHOLD

Experiments in comparative and clinical psychology have shown that deprivation, conflict, and severe frustration make organisms generally more irritable and aggressive. It is literally possible to change the "personality" of laboratory animals by subjecting them to such conditions. Closely analagous are the conditions of conflict under which many young people find themselves.

## INSECURITY AND DEFENSIVENESS

As previously noted, one method of gaining a feeling of importance is to identify with a group composed of other people who have similar yearnings and problems. A way to maintain the integrity of such groups or gangs, and at the same time to overcome one's own feeling of inadequacy, is to belittle others—to make fun of authority. In this respect the adolescent behaves as the member of a minority group (an in-group), with all the hostility and suspiciousness that goes along with such social arrangements.

## FEELINGS OF PERSONAL INADEQUACY

Closely akin to the mechanisms associated with insecurity and defensiveness are the reactions to real or imagined personal inadequacies. Young people who are handicapped by physique, appearance, or station in life may strike out at those whom they perceive to be more fortunate than themselves. They may act as if the world owed them something for the "dirty trick" it played on them.

The social and family conditions that are associated with youthful crime are perhaps even more clearly demonstrable than are the psychological ones. Following are some major correlates that have been associated with delinquency.

## ECONOMIC STRESS AND INSECURITY

Obviously, poverty per se is not a cause of delinquency, but the conditions of deprivation, of stress, or of family instability that are associated with it no doubt help to spawn delinquent behavior.

## FAMILY INSTABILITY

Delinquents' homes can be characterized as lacking good interpersonal relations, where discipline is either lax and erratic or unduly harsh, where there are contradictory values between parents or between the family and the social milieu in which it finds itself, and where there is either a lack of affection or, in extreme cases, downright hostility toward the child. Often such homes are "broken" by divorce or desertion.

## POOR OR INADEQUATE SCHOOL FACILITIES

The delinquent's troubles in school are more likely symptoms of his general difficulties than causes for his delinquency. It is known that delinquents do more poorly in school than non-delinquents, even when they are matched in ability. As might be expected, their records show more truancy, more dropouts, fewer clear-cut educational goals, fewer voluntary extracurricular activities, a greater history of misbehavior, and more transfers from one school to another.

The extent to which these school difficulties contribute to delinquency is not known. Unquestionably, they may add to the difficulties of an adolescent who is already "ripe" for striking out against the world. Many adolescents can find no place in the school. They are faced with a curriculum that offers them little chance for success and with a school social world that erects invisible but strong barriers to their participation.

## Prevention and Treatment

A great amount of work has been devoted to the study and prevention of delinquency. In nearly every large city in the country there are one or more programs aimed at solving this problem. In spite of this effort, the problem grows; the incidence of delinquency has continued to increase. This is not to say that the programs have been ineffective; indeed, some of them have yielded very good results. It simply indicates that these scattered programs (especially the intensive ones where real change has occurred) are as yet only a "drop in the bucket" when cast against the magnitude of the problem. The cost in time, effort, and money for dealing intensively with only a few of the thousands of problem cases to be found in a city is so great that most communities feel unable to bear it. Even if they were able, trained workers would not be available in sufficient numbers to handle the case load. What hope is there, then, that this problem can be alleviated? The answer lies in a broad program that embodies at least the following elements:

## EARLY PROGNOSIS

Already some success has been achieved through the early prognosis of delinquency. Three studies of delinquency—Sheldon and Eleanor Glueck's *Unraveling Juvenile Delinquency* (Commonwealth Fund); William C. Kvaraceus' *KD Proneness Scale* (New York; World Book Company); and New York City's Youth Board's *Delinquency Prediction, A Progress Report*—have shown means of early identification, even before the adolescent period. Except in high-delinquency areas, such specific predictive measures have not had widespread use. Their success, though, should indicate that more thorough records and diagnostic techniques would be valuable in all schools to point to adolescents with various problems (many latent), so that whether the problem is academic, emotional, or of a personality type, preventive measures could be taken while there was still a chance of success.

## TRAINING OF SCHOOL PERSONNEL

In the training of the average secondary school teacher, the topic of delinquency is covered in only about two or three pages of a textbook in educational psychology. Few ever take a course in juvenile delinquency, yet in some schools delinquents and potential delinquents make up a sizable portion of the classroom. The school counselor may have had a little more training. Social workers and school psychologists have probably had such training, but they exist in such small numbers that they do not even begin to fill the need for trained personnel in this area. At the very least, a beginning should be made to assure that all counselors and supervisory personnel receive education about juvenile delinquency. Along with the development of a core of personnel workers who know and understand the problem, teachers should receive solid work either as a special course or as a major unit of a course in adolescent psychology or educational psychology.

It should be re-emphasized that this is not an area of which we are ignorant. A great deal is known, and we have every reason to believe that such knowledge can be put to a useful purpose. It is, however, such an awesome problem, involving our whole social fabric, that schools are likely to say: "What can we do?" "Look at their homes." "Look where they live." "How can we change that?" So long as this attitude persists, it is unlikely that much progress will be made.

## CURRICULAR IMPROVEMENT

The near hysteria that followed Sputnik brought a wave of criticism of the American school. Within a few months some schools had already adopted a get-tough policy in grading, and within two years, Congress had appropriated large sums under the National Defense Education Act for the improvement of science and mathematics teaching. Programs thus improved represented some worthwhile progress in areas in which, as a society, we were already doing pretty well. Outmoded content in physics, mathematics, and biology began to be replaced, and teachers whose knowledge of their subjects was outdated were given financial support to take refresher courses. All this improvement was paralleled by an almost complete neglect of the other areas of the school, where we had not been doing well at all. In fact, the furor over improvements for the college-bound student may have actually led to a deterioration of programs for the underprivileged and culturally deprived adolescent. Many of the latter group still find little in most high schools that is commensurate with either their abilities or their vocational goals. Even if they do not drop out of school (many do, and they become excellent candidates for delinquency), they acquire little that will assist them in improving the wretched circumstances in which they find themselves. There is now a growing awareness of the need for a really comprehensive high school, including vocational and technical training, courses in functional English, mathematics, home economics, and social studies, as well as strong programs of remedial work for those who have not yet mastered such fundamental skills as reading, arithmetic, writing, and speaking.

## GROUP THERAPY AND COUNSELING

New York's program, called "Higher Horizons," in two slum-area schools gives convincing evidence that intensive counseling of culturally deprived adolescents can produce dramatic results. Although the aim of the program was to produce better schoolwork, there was also a decrease in delinquency.

The paucity of trained workers and the sheer expense of intensive individual counseling argues for the greater use of group counseling and therapy. Presently, however, there is little evidence that such programs are effective. Research is badly needed. It seems likely that a realistic program would include individual counseling (even including psychiatric care for the most seriously disturbed), with an adjunctive group-counseling program for the less seriously disturbed. One such program in a suburban school near Chicago, while not aimed at delinquency, did succeed in improving both the personal and social adjustment and the schoolwork of a selected group of academic underachievers.

## COMMUNITY IMPROVEMENT

Every major study of delinquency has shown a close relationship among living conditions, family and community instability, and delinquency. As already noted, teachers in slum-area schools may be so overwhelmed by the problems that children bring to school with them from their homes and neighborhoods that they react with almost cynical despair. It is, of course, naive to expect that a new housing-development program or a new school is going to solve the problem. In short, providing a psychologically unstable family with better material goods, while it may have a palliative effect, does not strike at the roots of the problem. Basic changes of attitudes and motives are required on the part of members of the community. Such changes are most effectively produced by the formation of community action groups in which adolescents are involved. The adolescent who is searching for

118     PSYCHOLOGY OF ADOLESCENCE FOR TEACHERS

significance, who has boundless energy and is not yet completely
cynical, may become the most valuable ally in any efforts that are
made toward better conditions of life.

## Readings for Further Study

Glueck, Sheldon, and Glueck, Eleanor T., *Unraveling Juvenile Delin-
quency*. Boston: Commonwealth Fund, 1950.
Havighurst, Robert J., *et al.*, *Growing Up in River City*. New York:
John Wiley & Sons, 1962, Chapter 6.
Healy, William, and Bronner, Augusta F., *New Light on Delinquency
and Its Treatment*. New Haven: Yale University Press, 1936.
Healy, William, and Bronner, Augusta F., "Treatment and What Hap-
pened Afterwards," *American Journal of Orthopsychiatry*, Vol. 14,
1944, pp. 33–34.
Kvaraceus, W. C., *Juvenile Delinquency and the School*. Yonkers-on-
Hudson: World Book Company, 1945.
Kvaraceus, W. C., *The Community and the Delinquent*. Yonkers-on-
Hudson: World Book Company, 1954.
*Juvenile Delinquency and the Schools*, Part I, 47th Yearbook of the
National Society for the Study of Education, 1948.
Redl, Fritz, and Wineman, David, *Children Who Hate*. Glencoe, Ill.:
Glencoe Free Press, 1951.

# The Psychological Foundations of Education Series

## Edited by VICTOR H. NOLL, Michigan State University

Intensive investigation in the field of educational psychology has resulted in the establishment of a wide variety of significant topics that warrant independent consideration. This paperbound series is designed to provide a deeper examination of specific areas which are not given thorough treatment in the many comprehensive textbooks now in use. It has always been necessary for teachers, on both undergraduate and graduate levels, to supplement the course text with specially prepared lectures or outside readings, and, in many cases, school library facilities are not adequately equipped to meet these needs. The volumes in the Noll series offer a convenient source of up-to-date and expertly written supplementary material. Teachers and students will benefit from the advanced coverage of pertinent subject matter. Used in conjunction with a comprehensive text, these books will increase the impact and effectiveness of current courses in the psychological foundations sequence. Theoretical material is an important part of each book, but emphasis is centered on practical applications.

## Initial Titles in the Series...

### PSYCHOLOGY OF ADOLESCENCE FOR TEACHERS

By GLENN MYERS BLAIR *and* STEWART R. JONES, *both of the University of Illinois*

A guide for prospective and in-service teachers, offering insight into the special problems encountered during the period of adolescence.

### PSYCHOLOGY OF THE CHILD IN THE CLASSROOM

By DON C. CHARLES, *Iowa State University*

A study of the particular needs and drives that motivate children during the elementary school years.

### GUIDANCE IN THE CLASSROOM

By RUTH STRANG, *University of Arizona, and* GLYN MORRIS, *Division of Guidance and Curriculum, Lewis County, New York*

Focuses on the role of the teacher and on guidance as an intrinsic part of teaching.

*Additional titles to be announced*

## The Series Editor:

VICTOR H. NOLL, (Ph.D., University of Minnesota), is Professor of Education at Michigan State University. Dr. Noll is co-editor of *Readings in Educational Psychology* and author *Introduction to Educational Measuremen*

THE MACMILLAN COMPANY, 60 FIFTH AVENUE, NEW YORK, N. Y. 10011

31063